ALTERNATIVE TO PARTITION

ALTERNATIVE TO PARTITION

*For a Broader Conception of America's
Role in Europe*

ZBIGNIEW BRZEZINSKI

*Prepared for the Atlantic Policy Studies Program
of the Council on Foreign Relations*

McGRAW-HILL BOOK COMPANY

New York   Toronto   London

Library of Congress Catalog Card Number: 65-20971

First Edition

08655

TO MUŠKA

Preface

The Cold War in Europe has lost its old meaning. There was a vitality and a passion to it as long as either side had reason to believe that it could prevail and as long as either side felt genuinely threatened by the other. Neither condition truly exists today. The West feels that it cannot undo by direct political action the communist regimes in East Europe, the division of Germany, and, most important of all, the Soviet presence on the banks of the Elbe. The communists, and particularly the Soviet leaders, now admit that there is no longer any reasonable chance for a communist revolutionary upheaval in the West. The two Soviet rebuffs suffered in Berlin in 1948–49 and again in 1958–62 have had much the same effect on communist expectations as the passivity of the West during the East German uprising of 1953 and the Hungarian revolution of 1956 have had on Western hopes.

Yet the status quo in Europe is far from satisfactory. The division of Europe on the Elbe is unnatural, unhistoric, and contrary to present trends favoring not only European economic and then political unification, but, most important of all, the rapidly spreading psychological sense of European unity. Hardly anyone in Europe, on either side of the river Elbe, is willing to argue that the division is in the interest of Europeans, and this includes increasingly even the Russians. It certainly is not in the interest of peace. Yet policies derived from past illusions, fears, and aspirations freeze both sides on the dividing line. Meanwhile, the danger mounts that the

East, frustrated ideologically, torn by internal divisions, will turn against itself, with the possibility of bitter national conflicts. The West at the same time becomes increasingly divided. Its former unity of purpose, born largely out of fear of Russian aggression, is dissipated in a destructive feud over priorities, objectives, and interests. Western spasms of resolve reinforce Soviet insecurity while Western irresolution reawakens Soviet offensive hopes. Both postures serve to perpetuate artificially and pointlessly the European partition.

How to bridge the gap dividing Europe without either side seeming to capitulate? How to achieve the restoration of Europe without creating new tensions in the process? These questions pose the central problem of the coming decade in Europe. With the internal pressures for change, accelerated by the Sino-Soviet dispute, surfacing in the Soviet Union and in East Europe, and with West Europe increasingly preoccupied with its identity, the division on the Elbe becomes more intolerable and the questions more urgent. Today Europe is still, to borrow De Gaulle's striking phrase, "without soul, without backbone, and without roots." But more and more Europeans, both eastern and western, are coming to resent this condition.

Indeed, the time has passed when Germany could be satisfied with a purely declaratory American policy on the issue of German reunification. The present internal trends in Germany, as well as general change in the European relationship to America, point clearly to the reemergence of the German issue as the key problem for U.S. policy, and the nature of the American response to it may determine the future American relationship to Europe. To be meaningful and effective, the American response will have to be based on a broader evaluation of the European scene, particularly with regard to the changes in the eastern bloc. The problem of the German partition has become critically linked to the problem of the European partition, and neither can be resolved without the resolution of the other.

It is the underlying thesis of this book that the creative initiative will have to come from the West, in particular from the United States. The East, still hampered by narrow ideological perspectives, cannot undertake to respond creatively to the emerging post–cold war conditions. Communist ideological erosion still lags behind European unification. The growing preoccupation of the Europeans with their destiny, however, offers the United States a unique opportunity to define a new objective behind which both America and Europe can join. A common venture infuses new unity. The goal of returning East Europe and Russia to the European civilization is capable of stirring European emotions and hopes, of giving West Europe a new commitment and of drawing East Europe with an irresistible magnet. Moreover, it is a goal that can be sought and eventually achieved in peace.

The argument in this book is addressed to all three audiences: To the Americans it argues that initiatives to promote elimination of the European partition are timely and essential—that American inaction may eventually prompt isolated West European ventures, born as much from resentment at America's passivity as from frustration with the continued division of Europe. To the West Europeans it argues that European initiatives alone will not suffice, that West Europe cannot by itself promote the climate of change, stimulate the pressures for unity, and finally provide the sense of security which will be necessary to attract East Europe and Russia. To the East Europeans and to the Russians it argues that the historical and ideological rationales for the division of Europe have been vitiated by political and economic developments of the last decade, and that true national security and territorial integrity can be sought and found in an all-European framework.

A secondary purpose of the book, but one closely related to the policy discussion, is to provide a general perspective on Soviet and East European evolution. The articulation of such a perspective seems to me especially desirable in the light of an emerging gap between the European (particularly West German) and American conceptions of the problems. As long as Russia was a direct threat to both America and West Europe, there was a seeming unanimity of views on both sides of the Atlantic. But the American-Soviet detente has contributed to an emergence of differing perspectives, with varying policy implications. It is hoped that the discussion that follows may contribute to bridging somewhat the existing gaps with respect to both analysis and policy.

The book is divided into two major parts. The first two chapters sketch descriptively and analytically the present political, social, and economic evolution of the eastern part of Europe. The first chapter focuses on the political fragmentation of the Soviet bloc and points to its domestic and international implications. The second chapter examines the decreasing effectiveness of the Iron Curtain, in spite of the efforts of communist governments to restrict closer contacts primarily to the economic realm. The remaining two chapters deal with policy issues. The third examines critically the European policies of the principal powers and concludes they not only fail to meet the needs of the times but are also in some respects even self-contradictory. The fourth and concluding chapter deals directly with policy recommendations, focusing on the need for a decisive American initiative.

This study was sponsored by the Council on Foreign Relations and, while the views expressed are my own, I benefited greatly by the counsel and experience of its members. I am also particularly grateful to Mr. John J. McCloy, the Chairman of the Board, and Mr. Harold van B. Cleveland, Director of the Atlantic Policy Studies Program, for helping to arrange high-level consultations in several key communist states as well as with various Western European leaders in Bonn, Brussels, London, and Paris. In addition, I derived many insights from consultations with high officials in Washington and from my participation in the last two

German-American Conferences and the 1962 Polish-American Roundtable.

In preparing this manuscript I revised and developed some of the ideas and policy suggestions that I previously published in *Foreign Affairs, The New Republic, The New Leader,* and elsewhere. In doing so, I was helped a great deal by the valuable comments and criticisms of Harold van B. Cleveland, William Diebold, Senior Fellow of the Council, George S. Franklin, Jr., Executive Director of the Council, William E. Griffith, Center for International Studies at M.I.T., Hans Speier, RAND Corporation, as well as of the various members of the Council's Atlantic Studies Steering Committee, chaired by Charles M. Spofford, and its advisory group on the Atlantic world's external environment, chaired by Eugene V. Rostow. In the preparation of the study I was ably assisted by Christine Dodson, who supervised the general execution of the project, and by Frances FitzGerald, Carole Parsons, Sophia Sluzar (who also assumed responsibility for preparing the index), and David Williams—all of whom at different stages helped me in research and in the preparation of tables, and by George Gilder, who edited the manuscript. As always, I have a special debt of gratitude to that vigilant and unrelenting critic, my wife.

Zbigniew Brzezinski

January 8, 1965

CONTENTS

"No army can withstand the strength of an idea whose time has come."

Victor Hugo

CHAPTER ONE

East Europe in Disarray

The partition of Europe is the consequence of fifty years of continental civil war. Europe's failure to organize itself, and wars among its nations, precipitated the entry into Europe of America and Russia, first as allies of the Europeans in fighting one another and eventually as the partitioners of Europe (the former center of the world) into two spheres of political and, more divisive still, ideological influence. The nations of Western Europe, with American encouragement, drew a lesson from their recent history and, in spite of occasional reversals, have gradually been moving toward a "European" solution to their historical dilemmas. East Europe, subordinated by Russia but not encouraged to stand by itself, has yet to find its way to Europe.

Europe in the Sixties

The disarray in communist Europe reflected the failure of Soviet leadership; the bickering in the Western alliance ironically testified to American success. The Soviet Union had failed in its objective of creating a stable communist empire in East Europe; the United States had succeeded in its quite different objective of fostering economic vitality and military security in the independent countries of West Europe.

Initially the Americans had hoped that all of Europe would participate in common recovery efforts. As a spur the Marshall Plan was made accessible to all the members of the anti-Nazi European alliance, and even to Italy and Germany.[1]

1

Its rejection by the Soviet Union and, under Soviet duress, by the other East European nations provided the foundations on which the Iron Curtain was erected and from which were launched the contrasting European policies of the two great powers.

Yet even after the rejection of the Marshall Plan, hope persisted that eventually all of Europe would undertake some common efforts. When NATO was established in 1949 it was designed by its architects as a temporary reaction to the division of Europe—not as an end in itself. In the meantime, by guaranteeing America's presence and commitment in Europe, NATO created the necessary atmosphere of security without which neither recovery nor unity would have been possible. Indeed, the quest for security against Soviet aggression was one of the major motives in the ready European acceptance of the American notion of interdependence between recovery and unity.

By the early sixties, however, the preoccupation with security had declined; right or wrong, most West Europeans no longer saw themselves threatened by Soviet invasion. This was why the new American-European dialogue could afford to evolve around alternative conceptions of military strategy and nuclear control. Revised official assessments in the West of the relative military strength of the two sides confirmed the new sense of European security, irrespective of any changes in Soviet ambitions and behavior. The decline in European insecurity paralleled European economic recovery, and both created an entirely new climate in American-West European relations, one in which the earlier automatic congruity of American-European interests became obscured by contradictory national priorities.

To France under De Gaulle America seemed to offer too little too late in response to French demands for a share in political leadership and nuclear power. A resurgent and an increasingly satisfied country, freed at last from colonial entanglements to pursue its "grandeur" by promoting a community of West European states that would be free of external political—and eventually military—direction, France sought "to end the American hegemony in Europe," as one of De Gaulle's cabinet members succinctly stated it.[2] For some Europeans, France's was thus the first effort to recreate a European hard core that would be free of both Soviet and American predominance, even if the initial price was the veto directed at England, seen by De Gaulle as an instrumentality of American penetration. For France, the kind of relationship that had prevailed in NATO since its creation had fulfilled its purpose: French security had been protected, and French recovery had been facilitated. The new stage could now be the reassertion of France's "grandeur" through leadership in the hard core of "liberated Europe"—i.e., the Common Market.

Initial American reaction was to minimize the significance of the change in Franco-American relations and to view it basically as a consequence of the personal, and hence transitional, impact of the French leader's personality. De Gaulle's various moves against NATO (the withdrawal of the French Mediterranean fleet, the refusal to integrate air tactical units, the recall of naval officers from headquarters, etc.) were presented to the American public as picayune pinpricks. They were not recognized as reflecting a deep-seated desire to weaken the instrumentality which De Gaulle saw primarily as a transitional means for the restoration of Europe—but which he felt with the passage of time had become almost an end of American policy. Little attention was devoted to the underlying causes of the shift in American-European relations; rather the tendency was to wait until the General disappeared, when the status quo ante would presumably be reestablished.

Unlike France, West Germany by the sixties was a resurgent but an unsatisfied country. For West Germany, the priorities had been different: security, internal democracy, membership in the West European community, unification, in that order, with some obvious overlap. By the late fifties all but the last had in some measure been achieved. This was precisely why the issue of unification began to assert itself in German political life. Until then, this issue had been obscured by other, higher priorities, even leading many observers to doubt that unification was in fact important to the Germans. It became fashionable to comment that the West Germans, complacently wealthy, were not really devoted to the idea of reunification— that the Christian Democratic Union feared the influx of seventeen million East Germans with their likely support for the Social Democrats. Leaving aside the inherent improbability that any major nation would willingly tolerate for more than two decades a foreign occupation of a significant portion of its people, much of the misconception about the extent of German concern was due to the priority wisely given by Adenauer to creating strong links with Western Europe and America. It was only by the late fifties, with the fading of German guilt feelings and a growing awareness of changes in East Europe, that reunification began to be item number one on the German agenda.*

Unlike De Gaulle, however, the Germans were not seeking to push America out of Europe. Their differing needs evoked different attitudes toward the United States. The Germans, too, were unhappy with the American tendency to make NATO and Atlantic unity an end in itself; but they stressed that NATO was there not only to provide Western security but also to seek European, or at least German, reunification.† These feelings were intensified by the American-Soviet detente after the Cuban confrontation. The American emphasis on the Atlantic partnership meant continued American leadership

---

* An EEC poll revealed in 1963 that a vast majority of Germans (81%) favored European integration and that 66% of the Germans considered reunification and the Berlin problem as the most important political issue, ahead of European unity. (*The Bulletin*, December 3, 1963). See also the emotionally charged article by R. Schroers, "Is There a Movement for Reunification?", *Merkur*, April 1962, and the lively discussions it produced in subsequent issues.

† Much of the initial impetus in Germany for Franco-German rapprochement was based on the misconception that together they would put pressure on Russia. De Gaulle, however, saw as his first priority pressure against America and only later by a continental Europe against Russia.

to the French and continued partition to the Germans. It presumed an identity of interests without an identity of goals. Yet, as Hans Morgenthau rightly observed, "Such identity of interests is rare in peace and cannot even be taken for granted in war. It exists among the members of the Atlantic alliance only on the most general plane: the Atlantic alliance is united in its opposition to communist aggression and subversion. But this interest is not a policy in itself: it must be implemented by common policies. Such policies, to which all members of the alliance are committed, do not at present exist." *

Accordingly, on both sides of divided Europe the lessened fear of war made particular national priorities more important in defining the attitude of each member state either toward NATO or toward the Warsaw Treaty. The degree to which the respective organizations, and especially their major sponsor powers, the United States and the Soviet Union, publicly recommitted themselves to, say, the cause of German reunification or the protection of the Oder-Neisse frontier had a direct bearing on the loyalty of Germany or Poland to the particular alliance system. Greater security also meant that Europe could again afford the "luxury" of ancient territorial feuds even among the members of each of the two hostile coalitions. The Albanian-Yugoslav dispute was a traditional nationality and tribal conflict, and so were the old feuds recently revived between two NATO members, Greece and Turkey.

The words "national sovereignty" were thus invoked with equal solemnity by General de Gaulle and First Secretary Gheorghiu-Dej, and by both with a feeling of security. They accurately perceived that while United States and Soviet military power had not declined, the two superpowers could not use it in any other way except to check each other. The French

---

* Hans Morgenthau, "The Crisis of the Western Alliance: An American View," *Commentary*, March 1963. The recent spate of books designed to prove the end of the Western alliance reflect the alliance's loss of purpose, the decline in the clarity of its goals.

leader's criticisms of the Atlantic Community as posing a threat to European independence—to the "very soul" of Europe—were matched by the Rumanian insistence that "socialist division of labor" was incompatible with the country's sovereignty. Gheorghiu-Dej's criticisms of tight integration might have been borrowed directly from De Gaulle.*

But much more important than these apparent parallels was the divergent thrust of historical development in the East and in the West respectively. West Europe, in spite of internal conflicts, is becoming more united; East Europe, with some of its nations even seeking contacts in the West to buttress their opposition to tighter integration, is becoming less united. The tradition of pragmatism and pluralism made it easier for the Western alliance to develop because it could absorb tensions and adjust to the notion of agreeing to disagree. In the communist system, there was an inherent inclination to "escalate" differences into matters of ideological principle, thereby inhibiting resolution of conflicts. As a result, differences in the communist world were treated as operations in political warfare and it was difficult to resolve them on the basis of compromise.

In East Europe reliance on narrow nationalism in resisting Soviet domination was often a substitute for either internal legitimacy or for external Soviet support. In West Europe even the French-inspired anti-American pressures in involved efforts to build closer ties among European nations. There was no parallel in East Europe to the Franco-German accord (including the amicable settlement of the Saar issue) and, what is much more important, there was no parallel to the development of a broader sense of community between the younger generations of West Europeans.[3] The decline of Soviet control over East Europe revealed that during the

* Even their policy of pinpricks against the former hegemones was similar: compare De Gaulle's pointed ignoring of the twentieth anniversary of the Normandy landing with Rumanian minimization of the Soviet role in the expulsion of the Nazis during the twentieth anniversary of that event.

period of Soviet domination little that was constructive was done to diminish traditional conflicts. At first, all East European nations were hermetically sealed off from one another; after Stalin, some were played off against others. This stood in sharp contrast to the widespread popular acceptance in Western Europe of the general notion of European unity,[4] backed throughout the postwar years by strong American support (even if later the idea in practice was partly turned against America). There was no equivalent in East Europe to the extensive and ramified movements promoting European unity and articulating the necessary ideas and programs,[5] and no parallel to EEC, which with its own "non-national" staffs and policy was a truly supranational organ.

During the period of international insecurity and economic recovery, an infrastructure of unity was built in Western Europe (WEU, Council of Europe, NATO, OECD, etc.) and the ability of the Common Market to survive even the unilateral French veto of the United Kingdom's entry, which so outraged the other members, was ironic testimony to the durability of the new fabric. In 1964 there was further progress toward merging the executive commissions of the three European communities—the Common Market, the Coal and Steel Community and Euratom—into a single board, and toward granting the European Parliament new budgetary responsibilities. Steps were taken to set up a contingency fund to be used when individual nations find themselves in sudden crisis. Late in 1964 the Common Market took the historic decision to set uniform agricultural prices for its members, despite the enormous difficulties involved.

In contrast, Stalin apparently had not thought it necessary to develop a multilateral institutional framework for his domination, and his successors found it difficult to create one in the context of simultaneous de-Stalinization and the Sino-Soviet conflict. It is revealing to note that the permanent staff for the Council of Economic Mutual Assistance (CEMA) was organized systematically only in 1963, and while EEC was a supranational body, CEMA clearly was not. Indeed, East European and Soviet economic cooperation, while gradually expanding, was still comparable only to the early stages of West European efforts at integration. Common banking and clearing facilities were only now being formed. Somewhat greater success was achieved in avoiding industrial duplication, but these efforts, as well as attempts at joint planning, were undercut by pricing difficulties and national jealousies (see below). As a result, there was an increasing tendency toward bilateral or more restricted regional arrangements. An example of the latter is the "Intermetal" project, involving joint administration of steel-rolling enterprises in Poland, Czechoslovakia and Hungary—a venture reminiscent of the Coal and Steel Community.

Even the most critical anti-American attitudes of some West Europeans were less intransigent than the bitterly strong and deeply ingrained anti-Russian nationalist feelings of many East Europeans. The American predominance during the first postwar decade in Europe was more acceptable to the West Europeans than the Soviet hegemony was to the East Europeans, because it did not involve direct territorial expansion and was effected by a power that was separated from Europe by the distance of an ocean. Given the nature of American politics, it did not involve the export of American ideological prescriptions to Europe, though most Americans did not conceal their preference for Dr. Ludwig Erhard's economic liberalism. (In fact, Americans urged Europeans to undertake cooperative economic planning on a scale which many of them would have found abhorrent in the United States.) The American approach, being less ideological, was less offensive, and much more cooperative. There simply was no parallel to the Stalinist pattern of domination and exploitation,[6] even if there was some truth in De Gaulle's assertion that America "wishing to help those who are in misery or bondage the world over, yielded in her turn to that taste for intervention in which the instinct for domination cloaked itself." [7]

True, to some it did seem that American postwar internationalism was still a projection of its prewar isolationism. The latter rejected the world, with its "foreign entanglements," because of the alleged inherent superiority of the American way. The former, with its desire to create a United States of Europe, involved an effort to reshape the world in the American image. Nonetheless, the efforts to spur European recovery through economic and eventually political European unity were compatible with the dominant mood prevailing in West Europe immediately after the war; Soviet domination in Eastern Europe was not. As a result, any Soviet conception of integration was automatically assumed to be a scheme for Russian domination—and the burden of proof to the contrary in the Eastern European view rested on Moscow. The underlying solidarity of the West, finally, was illustrated by De Gaulle's unequivocal support for the United States during the Cuban crisis.* The timidity and panic of the East European elites during those several days of tension must have provided the Soviet leaders with disconcerting evidence of the basic fragility of their structure.

Finally, in the Western alliance the major existing political and social systems, for all their internal ills and tensions, enjoy political legitimacy, reinforced by rapid improvement in the standards of living. Even the relatively high, but constant, communist vote in France and Italy testified to that legitimacy: it signified stable participation in the political game by parties that according to their theory ought to have been fomenting revolutionary upheavals. The inclination of these parties to speculate about "structural reforms" (à la Togliatti) and "peaceful revolution" not only reflected the internal bureaucratization of their leaderships, with the con-

---

* Thus De Gaulle was right when he asserted: "Thus if, once more, there are differences between Washington and Paris over the organization and functioning of the alliance, the alliance itself—that is, the fact that in the case of general war, France, with all means at her disposal, would be at the side of the United States, this being reciprocal, I believe—is beyond question. . . ." (Press conference of July 30, 1963).

sequent loss of revolutionary morale, but also their realization that anything more "activist" would simply deprive them of much of their popular support. This further contributed to the political legitimacy, and therefore stability, of the Western political systems.

In sharp contrast, the behavior even of the more generally moderate Polish and Yugoslav communist regimes, not to speak of the others, reflected the persisting lack of political legitimacy in East Europe. The restraints imposed on the intellectuals and the continuing denial of political democracy to the masses showed a realization by the ruling communist elites that both their rule, and to an even greater degree their ideology, had failed to gain popular acceptance.

The Europeans, both Eastern and Western, have not accepted the division of Europe. At the present this is still more a matter of mood than of political action. However, the growing power of EEC and the gradual shaping of common political institutions in West Europe make it almost inevitable that the political problem of East-West European relations will intrude heavily on the international agenda, especially since the abnormality of the European partition becomes increasingly less tolerable with the seeming normalization of East-West relations.

The Failure of Communist Internationalism

At the 1952 Congress of the Soviet Communist Party, the last one attended by Stalin, the relationship between the Soviet Union and the communist East European states was glowingly described as setting "an example of entirely new relations among states, relations never yet encountered in history." [8] Based on a common ideological outlook, these relations were alleged to guarantee the utmost respect for the sovereignty of the smaller East European states while assuring a common foreign policy.

The events of the decade or so which followed exposed

in full measure the failure of the 1952 pretentions. The very next year a rebellion erupted in East Germany, three years later Hungary was convulsed with revolution, and Poland and the Soviet Union were at odds. The Sino-Soviet conflict began in 1956–57 and culminated in violent mutual excommunications in 1963–64, with Albania unilaterally expelled from the communist bloc by the Soviet Union in 1961. Finally, the self-assertion of Rumania in 1963–64 testifies to the traditional character of the relations now prevailing among the communist states. Conflicts of economic interests, of political power, of ideological ambitions, and of national and territorial aspirations all have refuted the ideologically-rooted belief that "a new, socialist type of international relations arose with the formation of the commonwealth of socialist states. These are relations of fully equal rights, genuine friendship, fraternal cooperation in the sphere of politics, economics, and culture, and mutual assistance in the construction of a new life. These relations are determined by the nature of the social-economic system of the countries of the socialist camp; by the unity of their fundamental interests and ultimate great aim, the building of communism; and by the single Marxist-Leninist world view of the Communist and Workers' parties. . . ." [9]

The Soviet efforts to create in Europe east of the Elbe a united and stable interstate system based on the acceptance of Soviet leadership have failed. By 1964, with the exception of Ulbricht in East Germany and, to a lesser degree, Zhivkov in Bulgaria, East European communist leaders could no longer be considered pliant Soviet satellites. Each, in varying degrees, was becoming concerned with his own domestic power position and hence, inevitably, was growing more responsive to internal national pressures. Khrushchev's fall in 1964, removing from the scene an established leader with strong personal ties with most of the East European leaders, was bound to diminish further the stature of the Kremlin leadership. Of the eight formerly pliant satellites, by 1964 three had openly defied Moscow. The remaining five were loyal to Moscow but in varying ways and degrees. Broadly speaking, Gomulka supported Moscow out of self-interest and ideological preference; Ulbricht, out of political necessity; and Kadar, Novotny, and Zhivkov out of a combination of all three. Of the three defectors from Soviet control, by 1964 Tito was again allied with the Soviets, but this was largely a matter of Yugoslav decision, literally bought by persistent and costly Soviet wooing.

This wooing in some respects seemed worth the expense. The Yugoslavs, having recognized East Germany in 1957, supported the Soviet position that the German problem can only be solved by recognizing the "reality" of two German states, and in 1964 Tito helped Khrushchev by urging the Rumanians to restrain their self-assertiveness. The Yugoslavs even made their appearance as "observers" in several CEMA commissions and Yugoslavia became an associate member. The improvement in Soviet-Yugoslav relations also helped the Soviet Union in Africa and Asia, where Tito had developed reasonably good relations with such leaders as Nasser and Ben Bella. The Soviet decision to consolidate a close relationship with Tito was thus not only motivated by the need to eliminate an independent center of attraction in East Europe, but also by the desire to take advantage in the Middle East and Africa of Yugoslavia's standing and influence. But the price the Kremlin paid was historically important: the Yugoslav version of communism was legitimized and this was bound to influence Soviet relations with the other East European countries.

In part, a change in these relations was inevitable and even inherent in the original Soviet intentions. The Soviets always had a dual interest in controlling East Europe: first, it provided a defensive buffer and a strategically advanced jump-off point toward West Europe; second, it satisfied the ideological desire to create stable, and in the end, popularly accepted communist regimes in East Europe. What the Soviet leaders had not foreseen was that stable and popularly accepted regimes, even though communist, would tend to become nationalistic. It is no accident that the states that asserted their autonomy from Soviet control were predominantly the ones in which the communist regimes actually did gain political stability: Yugoslavia, Albania, and Rumania. Having effectively established their power by pushing radical Stalinist programs, they buttressed themselves by appeals to nationalism and insisted on their right to shape their own policies—in effect, to defy Moscow. The other East European states, less stable politically, have been more cautious either in domestic communization or in external self-assertion. Nevertheless, they too have become more confident in shaping policies according to their own felt needs and not purely in terms of Soviet priorities.

Much of the change in Soviet-East European relations was inevitable in that it came about simply because the passage of time gave the East European leaders greater confidence in ruling. But this natural process has been accelerated and intensified by the post-Stalin crisis in the communist world. Its initial symptoms were the Hungarian revolt and the return to power in Poland of Gomulka in 1956. These crises forced the Soviet leadership to reexamine its past exploitation and domination of the East European states and to attempt to define a new, more positive relationship with them. The reexamination became public in a Soviet declaration on October 30, 1956, and was followed by the extension of Soviet financial credits, designed to compensate for past abuses. Efforts were made to reinvigorate the hitherto dormant Council of Economic Mutual Assistance (CEMA) in the hope that economic interdependence, fostered by specialization and "socialist division of labor," would forge closer bonds of unity. Many multilateral political conferences were held among the leaders, designed to define new ideological principles of unity, based on a greater measure of equality. These initiatives might possibly have succeeded—even despite persisting internal East European economic difficulties, made more acute by the contrasting growth in the economic power and particularly in the standard of living of Western Europe, but for one decisive and simultaneous development: the Sino-Soviet dispute.

The impact of that dispute on the Soviet efforts to build a new structure of communist unity in Europe has been most destructive. By 1964 the dispute escalated from limited Chinese reservations in 1956 about the efficiency of Soviet leadership and disagreement in 1957 about foreign policies into a profound conflict over the very essence of the Marxist-Leninist ideology, over power and leadership in the entire communist movement, and finally even over Chinese-Russian territorial and economic interests. The relationship between the Sino-Soviet dispute and the Soviet-Albanian break is self-evident. But much more important has been the general effect of the dispute in making Eastern European support for Moscow so important to the Soviet leadership that the scope for maneuver and self-assertion by the East Europeans has been greatly enlarged.

Sometimes the maneuvering and self-assertion have been subtle and cautious—sometimes overt and dramatic. In Czechoslovakia, Novotny, hitherto a pliant tool of the Soviets, did not hesitate in 1962 to imprison a political rival, Rudolf Barak, a Minister of the Interior apparently popular among some Czech *apparatchiki,* who had hoped to advance his political career by imitating in Czechoslovakia the Soviet pattern of de-Stalinization. Barak was summarily arrested, publicly accused of political intrigues, and condemned to a lengthy prison term.* At the same time, Novotny stepped up the pitch

---

* Encouraged by Khrushchev's vigorous and public denunciations of Stalinism, made in late 1961 during the CPSU's XXII Congress, Barak, who had not been involved in the purge of Slansky and who earlier distinguished himself as a Khrushchev man by his vigor in attacking the Albanian leadership, clearly hoped to capitalize on the anti-Stalin wave by pressing in Prague for the rapid rehabilitation of the victims of the 1948–52 purges. Novotny, who had played a major role in these purges, must have perceived the political implications of Barak's initiative. See W. E. Griffith, *Albania and the Sino-Soviet Rift,* Cambridge, 1963, pp. 74–76, 141.

of his regime's denunciations of the Chinese and the Albanians. In effect, Moscow was told that internal Czech politics is one thing while external support is another. With the Albanian defiance a public success and with the Soviet-Chinese conflict intensified, Moscow had no choice but to acquiesce.

The Bulgarian leadership, similarly slow in its domestic de-Stalinization, did not welcome the Soviet efforts to have Bulgaria improve relations with Yugoslavia. The Bulgarian leadership, however, went along only reluctantly, despite persistent Soviet prodding, and it was evident that the formal improvement did little to heal old antagonisms. In 1964 the ancient Macedonian territorial issue was still simmering below the thin crust of superficially cordial relations.

The most dramatic act of self-assertion, significant in its immediate as well as potential consequences, was provided by Rumania. Its unfolding illustrated the subtle interrelationship between the tensions of the de-Stalinization process, continuing internal and regional economic difficulties, and the Sino-Soviet split. In an apparent effort to eliminate past "aberrations" in interstate relations, the Soviet government in 1958 removed its troops from Rumania. The Rumanian leadership, stably controlled by the trusted party leader Gheorghiu-Dej, had demonstrated steadfast loyalty during the critical days of October 1956. Yet the presence of this internally stable and effective leadership and the removal of direct Soviet leverage created the basic precondition for the subsequent successful act of defiance. The vehemence of Khrushchev's de-Stalinization had offended Rumania's still essentially Stalinist leaders and the clash between Soviet and Rumanian economic and political priorities, for which the Rumanian dislike of the Russians provided a historical underpinning, had caused further disaffection. Favorable circumstances for a defiant act were supplied by the Sino-Soviet conflict, with its immobilizing effect on the Kremlin's capacity to quell recalcitrant East European parties, and by the fact that Rumania's natural resources, especially oil, made it relatively immune to Soviet economic sanctions.

It is difficult to date precisely the beginning of serious Soviet-Rumanian dissensions, but they go back at least to the late fifties.[10] * One may assume that the orthodox Gheorghiu-Dej and his colleagues (since 1952 the Rumanian leadership has been remarkably homogeneous and unchanged in composition in comparison to some of the other East European politburos) were rather disconcerted by the increasing Soviet toleration for Gomulka's revisionist agricultural policies, at a time (in the early sixties) when the Rumanians were scrupulously completing a harshly enforced collectivization drive. Moreover, they must have been unfavorably impressed by the extent to which the Soviet leadership had used economic sanctions in its futile efforts to bring the defiant Albanian leadership to its knees. Accordingly they were skeptical about various proposals for a closer economic integration of the communist states.

In September 1962 Khrushchev, in a published article,[11] called openly for the setting up of a supranational planning authority, for common investments in the development of supranationally owned enterprises, and for supranational coordination of investment plans.[12] The proposal's implementation would have closely integrated all the East European economies with the USSR, giving the latter, with its size and resources, greatly increased economic leverage. Khrushchev was supported primarily by East Germany and Czechoslovakia, the two most developed and politically most orthodox communist states. A more rational division of labor and a tighter integration of long-range plans would ensure stable markets for the export of machinery made in these countries;

---

* Just as in the past there was a tendency in the West to minimize all bloc conflicts, there is now an inclination to review all previous signs of friction and to conclude from them that the conflicts that subsequently developed were both inevitable and had in fact commenced almost immediately in the postwar years. However, many of these frictions could have been sustained if not for the disruptive effects of the Sino-Soviet conflict and the post-Stalinist transformation.

When the Sino-Soviet conflict reached its peak of reciprocal abuses early in 1964, the Rumanians first offered themselves as go-betweens, thereby forestalling for two months a planned public attack on Peking by Khrushchev. This initiative at "mediation" was presumably motivated by the Rumanian interest in preserving the Sino-Soviet "divergent unity," which gave them maximum room for maneuver without having to choose sides. As mediators, moreover, the Rumanian leadership was automatically elevated from the position of a minor member of the Soviet-dominated sphere into an independent, even though smaller, partner, passing judgment on the behavior of the two major communist powers. The Rumanians thus could defy Moscow with impunity and this they did—with obvious relish. Shortly afterwards, Bucharest issued a remarkably vehement public declaration (April 27, 1964), arrogantly criticizing both the Chinese and Soviet behavior, vigorously rejecting the Soviet prescriptions for CEMA, and asserting emphatically the Rumanian right to independence in all policies.

The comments on CEMA and communist interstate relations were especially damaging to the Soviet effort to build its own community in Europe. Supranational management and planning bodies were bluntly described as "not in keeping with the principles which underlie relations among the socialist countries. The idea of a single planning body for all CEMA countries has the most serious economic and political implications . . . superstate or extrastate bodies would make of sovereignty an idea without any content." The Rumanians stressed their determination to "develop [Rumania's] economic links with all states irrespective of their social system" and noted, with a touch of irony probably meant for the East Germans and the Czechs, that "undoubtedly, if some socialist countries

their own needs and potentialities. You bully those fraternal countries whose economies are less advanced and oppose their policy of industrialization and try to force them to remain agricultural countries and serve as your source of raw materials and as outlets for your goods."

thus they argued that the less developed states should integrate even more than they.*

Rumanian resistance to Khrushchev's schemes was evident at the December 1962 session of CEMA, held in Bucharest, and some reservations were shared by other member-states, presumably fearful that Khrushchev's plans would encroach too much on their already limited independence. The Rumanians may have also been emboldened by the loss of prestige suffered by Moscow during the Cuban crisis. They stiffly opposed the Soviet view, supported by the more industrially developed East Germany and Czechoslovakia, that the "division of labor" in the communist world should proceed on the "principle of efficiency," which meant in effect that the less industrially developed nations, such as Rumania, should be satisfied with slower industrial development and with providing the raw material base and the agricultural support for the industrially more developed countries.

The Rumanian response was indignant, springing from years of resentment over past exploitation.† As a Rumanian spokesman said: "Just as on the domestic scene an absolutist criterion of efficiency cannot be countenanced, so in the field of specialization and cooperation between the socialist countries economic efficiency and profitability cannot be accepted

* The Czechs also must have been mindful of the dislocations caused in their economy by the sudden cancellations of orders for Czech machinery in the middle fifties and early sixties by the Poles and the Chinese respectively, while the East Germans probably recalled the difficulties produced by the precipitous decline in the Polish deliveries of bituminous coal in 1956–57. In both cases, the motives for these unilateral actions were political in origin—the Polish decision to abandon the Stalinist economic policy and the Chinese to cut their economic links with the Soviet bloc. Presumably, the Czechs and the East Germans hoped that closer ties would reduce such hazards. For a further discussion, see J. M. Montias, "Uniformity and Diversity in the East European Future," (unpublished paper, 1964). A most informative discussion of CEMA problems, held by East European and Soviet economists, is contained in Nos. 4 and 6, 1964, of *The World Marxist Review.* Rumanian objections are stated frankly and openly discussed by the others.
† J.M. Montias, "Uniformity and Diversity . . ." suggests that Rumanian opposition to the Soviet integration schemes was reinforced by arguments referring to past Soviet exploitation of Rumania which, he suggests, "was more oppressive . . . than in any other country of Eastern Europe" (p. 14).

as the one and only criterion with which to evaluate new economic steps." And he asserted: "Building communism on a world-wide scale is incompatible with the notion of dividing countries into industrial states and agrarian states, into developed countries and underdeveloped countries."[18] Other Rumanian economists explicitly attacked their East German colleagues for having suggested that less developed communist countries like Rumania should practice "passive industrialization," i.e., one which is merely a byproduct of over-all economic growth and not the consequence of conscious policy. This clearly went against Gheorghiu-Dej's Stalinist grain. The East German economists were even accused of actually imitating capitalist economists.*

Three factors made it difficult for Moscow to respond effectively to the Rumanian opposition. One was the development of Western Europe, which, on the one hand, involved the rapid industrial development of a relatively backward country such as Italy (thereby creating an embarrassing example) and, on the other, could present the Rumanians with tempting trade arrangements (which by 1963 was increasingly being done).† The second involved internal economic difficulties in the Soviet Union and East Europe, resulting from agricultural failures, from the incapacity of the systems to meet rising consumer demands, and from the pressures for higher military appropriations precipitated by the Berlin crisis provoked by the Soviets in the years 1958–62. The Soviet agricultural failures had produced planning complications for the more in-

* C. Murgescu, "Pseudo-theories Which Try to Drain Industrialization of Its Content," *Viata Economica*, August 23, 1963. The author also ridiculed the Economic Institute of the East German Academy of Sciences for suggesting that the "smaller" countries be the ones to practice "passive industrialization" by observing that in fact East Germany is smaller than Rumania! A year later the Rumanian economist returned to the attack, violently criticizing the East Germans again for recommending intensified CEMA specialization, with the Rumanians urging instead a looser structure including even China (*Viata Economica*, June 5, 1964).

† E.g., in November 1962 an Anglo-French consortium underwrote the $39 million construction of the steel rolling mill in Galati, a project dear to the Rumanian leadership and one the Soviets had discouraged.

dustrially developed East European states, forcing purchase grain from the West. This new economic made them even less anxious to use their resources industrialization of the agrarian communist states. T was the intensification of the Sino-Soviet crisis, with plications within the communist world. The Chinese, accurately the mood not only in Rumania but also in and Hungary,* pointedly raised the matter of discrim economic development in their attacks on Moscow: "V that it is necessary to transform the present Council nomic Mutual Assistance of socialist countries to acco the principle of proletarian internationalism and to tu organization, which is now solely controlled by the lea the CPSU, into one based on genuine equality and benefit, which the fraternal countries in the socialist can join of their own free will."[14] The Rumanians demonstr republished some of these attacks in their own press. was little Moscow could do about this. Direct military in view of the earlier Soviet withdrawal from Rumania, have had to be a direct invasion. Political pressure migh backfired and even precipitated a Rumanian endorsem the Chinese, which the Chinese were clearly seeking.†

* The sense of apprehension in East Europe was revealed by frequent pre ments designed to pacify public opinion. The following from the Hungarian tion *Figyelo*, May 27, 1964, is typical: "The process of economic inte among nations causes in many people 'concern' about national sovereignty. it would be worthwhile to try to examine the problem more closely. The q is whether a country is economically independent only if it relies entirely own resources and prepares its economic plans accordingly, whether a cou independent only if it covers out of its own resources the demand for all imp goods. It is not difficult to answer this question. There is not one single c anywhere in the world which could develop equally every branch of its ind which could cover both its demand and supply of every product out of do production. . . . An interpretation of national sovereignty based on self-suffi is not only senseless, but also unnecessary. In our opinion, a certain degr economic dependence is by no means in contradiction with national econ sovereignty."

† Thus the Chinese letter to Moscow of February 29, 1964, subsequently public by Peking, clearly had the Rumanian reactions in mind when it st "You infringe the independence and sovereignty of fraternal countries and o their efforts to develop their economy on an independent basis in accordance

see fit to adopt forms of cooperation in direct relations different from those *unanimously* agreed upon within CEMA, that is a subject which exclusively concerns those countries and can be decided by them alone in a sovereign way" (italics added). Shortly afterwards, the Rumanians signed a favorable economic agreement with the United States.

On the broader subject of relations among communist states, the Rumanians were equally unequivocal. In a remark pointedly aimed at the Soviet inclination to equate their own good with the good of the communist world, they noted that "no specific or individual interests can be presented as general interests, as objective requirements for the development of the socialist system." They openly criticized past Soviet practices which had gone "as far as the removal and replacement of leading cadres and even of entire central committees, as far as imposing leaders from without, the suppression of distinguished leading cadres of various parties, as far as censuring and even dissolving communist parties." The Rumanian statement left no doubt that in its view both domestic and foreign policies were "each party's exclusive right" and that "no party has or can have a privileged place, or can impose its line or opinions on other parties."

The defiant tone of the Rumanian declaration was underscored by its issuance a mere three weeks after an eloquent personal plea by Khrushchev for greater interdependence in the communist Euro-Asian community. Speaking on April 3 in the course of his visit to Hungary, the Soviet leader had urged more coordination among CEMA and Warsaw Treaty countries, not only on economic matters but also on foreign policy. The Rumanian stand was a drastic setback for the Soviet effort, which was supported in varying degrees by the Czechs, East Germans, and, particularly on investments, by the capital-short Poles, to use CEMA as a framework for communist unity. The Rumanians instead advanced the proposition—almost the opposite of the Soviet view—that each nation must first prepare its own economic plan before engaging in bilateral and multilateral arrangements with others. It was ironic to think that the Soviet spokesmen in the past had frequently cited the principle of unanimity in CEMA's operations as proof that international communism inherently respects national sovereignty. The Rumanians, by asserting their right to veto, demonstrated that national sovereignty can frustrate common communist policies.

Although the Rumanian position provoked initial irritation and hostility among the other CEMA members, it was bound to be contagious in its long-range effects. The Rumanians, like De Gaulle in the West, were setting their national interest above the broad "common" interest of other like-minded states. They most certainly were not defecting to the other side, unless pushed there by excessive reactions from the dominant power of their bloc. But they were rejecting the notion of an integrated community of the ruling Euro-Asian communist parties and openly urging instead a looser community of communist states. Their success demonstrated the decreasing significance, as a political asset, not only of Soviet military power * but also of geography. Although surrounded by pro-Soviet communist states, the Rumanians defied the communist equivalent of "the principle of geographic fatalism"—that to defy the USSR one must at least enjoy the advantage of geography.† The availability of timely Western alternatives (the American-Rumanian agreement was initialed

---

* The Soviet Union was learning in East Europe what the United States had learned earlier in Central America: military power is a declining political resource in conflict with small powers, except under condition of a more generalized threat to the interests of the major power (e.g., the Soviet reaction in 1956 in Hungary was in large measure designed to save the entire bloc from disintegrating). Paradoxically, however, Soviet military might has given recalcitrant East European communist elites a sense of security. Since the crumbling of the communist regime would constitute a net gain for the West, even isolated Albania found itself protected from any Western-supported invasion by Soviet deterrent power.

† The communists have long held the theory, finally refuted by Cuba, that communist revolutions in isolated regions, far removed from the communist world, will inevitably be crushed by the "imperialists." Until Rumania, cases of defiance of Moscow involved countries like Yugoslavia, or Albania, not to speak of China, which were not subject to Soviet or pro-Soviet encirclement.

in Washington on June 1, barely over a month after the Rumanian declaration) also contributed to the long-range contagion of the Rumanian stand,* and increased East European pressure on Moscow for more aid.†

There is ample reason to believe that by mid-1964 the Rumanian stand, as well as the Soviet and Western reactions to it, were being carefully reviewed in the other East European capitals. Should the Rumanians succeed in promoting—and even accelerating—their economic development, while also increasing and protecting their independence from Soviet control, their example would prove attractive to the other elites, even if some of the economic motivations of the Rumanians (including their Stalinist pro-industrial biases) should be absent elsewhere.

The Rumanian example may be especially appealing because it was a classic in graduated defiance. It was not the consequence of sudden domestic turmoil, as in Poland in 1956, nor of a sudden expulsion, as that of Yugoslavia in 1948. It was a matter of gradual self-assertion, which could hardly justify a violent reaction. In early June 1964, after the Washington agreement, a top level Rumanian delegation was cordially received in Moscow, showing that, despite a brief flurry of Soviet-Rumanian radio polemics,‡ the Soviet leaders de-

---

* The spate of articles in the East European press, published in early 1964, designed to prove that autarky is *not* a good idea and that economic cooperation is most desirable, was an attempt to minimize the Rumanian appeal. The reactions of the Polish press and numerous queries from readers, testified to the interest the Rumanian behavior aroused. See *Zycie Warszawy*, June 26, 1964, or *Polityka*, June 27, 1964, both trying to minimize the Rumanian development.

† Typical is the Hungarian view, expressed by L. Hay, "Notations Concerning Equalization of Economic Levels," *Kozgazdasagi Szemle*, August 1964, which demanded more help for Hungary's development, and complained of inadequate help from CEMA countries.

‡ Shortly after the Rumanian statement, and especially after the Rumanian-American economic agreement, Radio Moscow's Rumanian broadcasts began to attack those who "say that socialist cooperation leads to the transformation of certain countries into raw material or agricultural dependencies, thus leading to a loss of their equal status and political independence. This cannot be appraised otherwise than as a deliberate distortion of the character of economic relations between socialist countries." (Radio Moscow, May 30, 1964.)

The Bucharest radio responded vehemently, particularly subjecting to ridicule

cided to treat gently their self-assertive neighbors. This seemed to prove that measured self-assertion results not in Soviet sanctions but in greater Soviet respect.

Further pressures in East Europe for more autonomy —and eventually complete independence—could also be stimulated by intensified Chinese mischief-making. In the summer of 1964, the Chinese made the first open effort to capitalize on European territorial conflicts by pointing to Russian expansion at the cost of Finland, Poland, Rumania, and Germany, and also to the Polish acquisition (balancing Polish losses to Russia) of the Oder-Neisse frontier.[15] Other Chinese efforts may follow. For example, a public endorsement by Peking of the Bulgarian claims to Yugoslav Macedonia would inescapably spark nationalist-inspired pro-Chinese sentiments in Sofia while facing Moscow with a Hobson's choice: support for the Chinese provocation would be unthinkable, given the Soviet stake in good relations with Belgrade; yet Soviet equivocation, not to speak of opposition, would further complicate Zhivkov's internal position, undermining his unpopular policy of Yugoslav-Bulgarian rapprochement. Other opportunities for Chinese intrigue exist in the old and bitter Transylvanian conflict, intensified since 1958 by Rumanian repression of the Hungarian minority; in the Czech-Slovak antipathies; and even in nationality problems in the Soviet Union itself. By reawakening old hostilities, the Chinese can resume the time-tested game of playing one European nation against another.*

International politics have returned to East Europe and, by the same token, East Europe is returning to international politics. The cumulative thrust of recent developments points

---

Moscow's criticism of the Washington-Bucharest agreement. It noted that trade with the West had been personally backed by Khrushchev and was being developed by the USSR. (Radio Bucharest, June 5, 1964.)

* The demonstrative Chinese rejection of Khrushchev's early 1964 "border freeze" proposal may not be unrelated to these long-range calculations, in addition to the more immediate concern over the Sino-Soviet frontier dispute. For public evidence of Rumanian-Hungarian quarrels on the old territorial issues, see C. Daicoviciu, "Debate of Historians," *Contemporanul*, May 25, 1964, reporting sharply contrasting versions of Transylvanian history.

unmistakably in the direction of accelerating nationalist self-assertion in the definition of Eastern European domestic and foreign priorities.* Rumania, and earlier Albania and Yugoslavia, had asserted their external independence of Moscow by initially combining domestic Stalinism with nationalism. Their stand fractured communist unity. Poland, Hungary, and, more lately, Czechoslovakia have moderated and liberalized the earlier harshness of communist rule while maintaining close relations with Moscow. Their evolution also contributed to a gradual erosion of communist ideological militancy.

The return of international politics to East Europe has increasingly tended to restrict Soviet freedom of action in Central Europe. It is doubtful that the East European elites were happy to see the Berlin issue reopened in late 1958 in such a precipitate fashion by Khrushchev. With the threat of war seemingly acute, panics actually took place during 1961 in several East European cities, and the ruling elites were clearly uneasy over the sudden display of Soviet brinkmanship, which afforded no obvious benefit to themselves while exposing their countries to West European MRBM's (Medium Range Ballistic Missiles). Even the possibility of conventional conflict in Central Europe panicked the populations, created economic dislocations, and produced a general mood of insecurity. For Prague or Warsaw, the issue was satisfactorily resolved by the wall erected in August 1961, which shored up the buffer East German regime. The maintenance of the status quo in Germany was preferable to any change in the situation; a united communist Germany was no more welcome than a united NATO Germany. Moreover, the success of the Rumanian defiance and the emerging opportunities for more independent initiatives either toward the West or China gave the East European states a greater sense of confidence in pursuing their interests as they saw them. They were in a better position

---

*In the summer of 1964, asked by the writer to define "communist internationalism," an East European communist leader replied unequivocally: "Helping our own welfare, not anybody else's."

to hint to Moscow that they might not be able to guarantee either diplomatic or military backing for any precipitate Soviet moves. Their stake in stability in Central Europe thus was bound to limit Soviet freedom of action.*

A more immediate practical consequence of the priority given to domestic self-interest over broader communist goals was the increasing isolation of East Germany from the rest of East Europe. During 1963 and 1964, the Federal German government, taking advantage of the persisting economic difficulties of several East European states and of the inability of the USSR to meet their investment needs, succeeded in negotiating trade agreements with Poland, Hungary, Rumania, and Bulgaria in which the East Europeans, after some initial hesitations, finally acceded to the West German formula linking West Berlin to the formal agreement.† As a consequence, West German trade missions, with modified diplomatic status, were established in the East European capitals, representing West Germany and West Berlin.

These agreements were concluded in the face of many East German public warnings that the West German government was pursuing aggressive and subversive goals and that the inclusion of West Berlin in the agreements was aimed at East Germany.‡ In the spring of 1964, the East Germans,

---

* Interesting in its implications was the very warm reception given in Warsaw to the Finnish President Kekkonen. One may wonder whether the Poles were not thinking of themselves when their head of state, A. Zawadzki, stated: "We appreciate the significance and advantages flowing from the neutrality of Finland, both for itself and for other countries. In particular we highly appreciate your outstanding role, Mr. President, in the realization and activation of the foreign policy of your country. A distinct expression of this policy and at the same time an example of peaceful coexistence of states with different systems are the neighborly and mutually advantageous relations between Finland and the Soviet Union." (Radio Warsaw, March 3, 1964.)

† Thereby implicitly refuting the Soviet "three German states" concept.

‡ See *Neues Deutschland,* November 16, 1963; February 13, 1964. The East German protests over the Polish-West German agreement were sharply rebuked by the Poles: "It is not our task at the moment to analyze the West German reasoning and to what extent the new three-year agreement, together with the setting up of the West German trade mission provided for in that agreement, fits into the framework of certain Bonn political doctrines. . . ." (*Trybuna Ludu,* editorial, March 13, 1963.)

apparently supported by the Soviets,* launched a comprehensive campaign against the West German strategy, said to be based on "the illusion of being able to weaken the close relations of the GDR with some people's democracies, first by economic and later on by other means." [16] Ulbricht, in the course of a visit to Hungary, warned of the West German economic "Trojan horse" designed to "disturb relations among the Warsaw Pact countries" and directly told the Hungarians: "In this connection, I would like to stress that in fact and in law the whole of Berlin is situated on the territory of the GDR." [17]

In seeking to avoid isolation in East Europe, the East Germans found solace in an unexpected quarter: Yugoslavia. In 1957 Belgrade had been persuaded by Gomulka that its influence in the eastern bloc would be increased if there were diplomatic relations between Belgrade and Pankow. In retaliation, Bonn, enforcing the Hallstein doctrine, suspended diplomatic relations with Yugoslavia. Subsequently, various minor incidents contributed to further acrimony between Yugoslavia and West Germany, and the East Germans, eager to capitalize on this, made extensive efforts to develop their trade with Yugoslavia.† Nonetheless, even the East German-Yugoslav rapprochement reflected further differentiation in the previously monolithic conditions. Seeking support from the most independent communist country in East Europe is hardly a step toward communist unity; it reflected the return of international politics to an area which for more than a decade had been restricted to bilateral and rather unequal relations with Moscow.

The new East German professions of admiration for the Yugoslav regime, furthermore, were bound to strengthen in-

* According to *Frankfurter Allgemeine Zeitung*, May 15, 1964, at the Geneva World Trade Conference the Soviet delegation urged the conferees not to permit the Berlin clause in any agreements with the Federal German Republic.
† East German-Yugoslav trade by 1970 is scheduled to triple the 1964 level of approximately 400 million marks, which was already an increase of 10% over the 1962 level.

ternal pressures against Ulbricht and his oppressive policies. Demands for at least partial imitation of the Yugoslav experiment gained ideological legitimacy and could no longer be dismissed as evidence of "revisionism." Yet since to liberalize one-fourth of a country is probably four times as difficult as the liberalization of any single East European country, Ulbricht's regime continued to face the dilemma that any internal relaxation almost automatically tended to reopen public discussion of the problem of German unity. Yugoslav support was a very mixed blessing.

Since communist states still prefer to associate themselves with other communist states, the new pattern represents a transformation of the relations among them, not a total separation. Yugoslavia broke away and then returned as a junior ally rather than as a docile satellite of the Soviet Union. In 1956 Gomulka asserted Polish independence from Soviet control; subsequently, he returned to a closer but more autonomous relationship with the Soviet Union. Rumania is not defecting to the West; it has, however, taken advantage of the new condition of diversity and conflict within the communist community to improve its bargaining position and even to assert its right to deal independently with the West.

The pattern of change means the revival of the supremacy of states and the reappearance of state to state relations; it means the collapse of the old communist dream of one united communist state. The Soviet leadership failed to capitalize on a historical opportunity to impose an international solution in the late forties when it could have done so; its bumptious and precipitous policies, its reliance on ideological excommunication and economic sanctions (as toward Albania) merely stimulated nationalist reactions. What Stalin felt he need not do or perhaps even could not do, namely, to forge the people's democracies into a single coordinated political and economic system, his successors certainly will not be able to do. Stalin did not create stable foundations for an enduring empire; Khrushchev did not develop the style of international leadership. East Europe is where the dream of communist internationalism lies buried.

The Conflicting Pulls of the Domestic Priority

The return of international politics to East Europe increased the importance of domestic factors in shaping the behavior of East European governments. Domestic difficulties, both economic and political, compelled the ruling communist elites to give priority to their domestic needs in their bargaining with the Soviet Union. This was facilitated by such extraneous circumstances as the complications of the de-Stalinization campaign, the Sino-Soviet conflict, and the willingness of the West to give the East European regimes new options. Increased room for maneuver and the elites' own sense of greater national identification impelled them to put a higher premium on domestic support, eroding the formerly common ideology with its international priorities.

Conditions varied from country to country. Some previously more moderate, such as Poland, seemed in some respects—particularly in policies toward the intellectuals and the church—to be adopting retrograde measures; others previously more repressive, such as Hungary and Czechoslovakia, were adopting more liberal policies. But throughout East Europe, Marxism-Leninism, either as a guide to socio-economic activity or as a system of thought, was clearly on the defensive and undergoing an accelerating erosion. Its historical irrelevance in agrarian economies was illuminated by the failure of collectivization, and in highly industrial ones, by Czech economic problems. Vigorous cultural debates,*

* For example, see the outspoken statement by Professor Fritz Cremer, sculptor, at the Fifth Congress of the Association of German Creative Artists in East Berlin, as reported by the *Frankfurter Allgemeine Zeitung*, May 6, 1964; the outspoken comments by Czechoslovak intellectuals, including the defiance of the Czechoslovak Central Committee by the editorial staff of the magazine *Kulturny Zivot* (particularly their editorial of May 1, 1964, entitled "We Still Have Our Tasks and Our Pens") and the outbursts by party spokesmen, particularly L. Stoll, "Is It Merely the Subjectiveness of Different Generations That Is Involved?",

outspoken economic revisionism, public demands for humanism,* and widespread preoccupation among the youth with Western leisure and mass culture, all highlighted a growing awareness of ideological obsolescence.[18] Economic revisionism often went so far as to impugn the most fundamental Marxist concepts,† and it was manifest in efforts to rationalize and decentralize planning and management.

None of this should be construed as reflecting a positive desire for the prewar political and social structure or for capitalism. In most cases, the dissatisfaction and frustration lacked a sense of a positive political alternative, though when pressed, most East Europeans, with the exception of the ruling groups, usually stated their preference for the Swedish or Finnish social democratic model. Many showed interest in the new Christian Democratic programs of socio-economic reforms, while the growing problem of urban delinquency increased the preoccupation with morality and ethics. But if anything in general seemed to attract the young people, it was

---

Rude Pravo, April 26, 1964; the defense of Western creative writing heard at the Rumanian Writers Union Executive Committee Session at its March 1964 sessions, including open attacks on political priority in esthetic assessments, with the writer Ion Ianosi noting that: "It would be unfair to reduce the literature of a capitalist country to its left-wing representatives, just as it would be unfair to ignore the part played by these elements in the country's literary development, having advanced political convictions is not the sole guarantee for attaining literary value. . . ." (*Gazeta Literara*, April 9, 1964.) In Hungary, the cultural life became so open that the ideological watchdogs expressed growing concern over the penetration of Western values and over persisting anti-Soviet nationalist feelings, even though they warned the party *apparatchiki* against reverting to their old "prejudices against the intelligentsia" and particularly against past practices, in handling oppositional views. (P. Renyi, "Ideological Work and the Intelligentsia," *Tarsadalmi Szemle*, November 1963.)

* The old East German communist, Professor Robert Haveman, brought on himself many attacks by East German *apparatchiki* for a series of outspoken lectures demanding that socialism be imbued with humanism and criticizing past communist practices.

† Including such statements as, "When someone criticizes some measures today, some person will say, 'This far you can go. But you try to criticize socialism as a social order!' But I do indeed believe that it is necessary that we begin to criticize socialism as a social order." Z. Haba, *Hospodarski Noviny*, Nos. 45–46, 1964. For a good over-all analysis, see Michael Gamarnikow, "The Growth of Economic Revisionism," *East Europe*, May 1964.

the vague idea of European unity, usually defined more in cultural and social than in political terms. The desire to travel freely, to be part of the European adventure, to share fully in its civilization and growth—that seemed to be a strong feature of the restless rejection by East European youth of the dogmas and ideological slogans of their ruling elites.*

The elites had relatively little to say in response. The old ideologues were discredited and silent, or themselves increasingly revisionist. The party Agit-Prop officials were groping for some persuasive explanations for the Sino-Soviet dispute that theoretically should never have arisen among "brotherly" communist states. The leaders, realizing that they needed closer economic contacts with the West, were hard put to find effective ways of avoiding "ideological exposure" to the contagious principles and way of life of the West, and were haunted by the specter of European unity.

The internal political condition of several of the East European communist elites could be summarized by the words "factional conflict" and "ideological demoralization." The factional conflicts had many roots. Some were prompted by the approaching imminence of a struggle for succession. Ulbricht and Tito were in their seventies; the other leaders were around sixty. Their political lieutenants had inevitably to give thought to their own political prospects, and the maneuvering and shadowboxing involved in the presuccession crisis was thus underway. A more general phenomenon was the growing conflict of generations. The old underground communist and the Moscow-trained *apparatchiki* were slowly giving way to the domestically trained and domestically reared young communist *apparatchiki*. Few of them were fanatical,

* In mid-1964 high East German officials were forced to explain publicly at length why the East German youth cannot travel throughout Western Europe. See the belabored explanation by Gerhard Eisler, *Neues Deutschland*, May 14, 1964, as well as Ulbricht's speech in Budapest, May 11, 1964, in which he explained why East Germans are more restricted in their travel than Hungarians. The irrelevance of communist appeals was strikingly demonstrated by a series of public opinion polls taken among the Polish youth in the years 1957–61. More recently, the government has not permitted coverage of such sensitive subjects by the public opinion polls.

dedicated Marxist-Leninists; most often they were just concerned with acquiring positions of power and dealing with immediate policy issues. The conflict for power frequently exaggerated differences over policy.

Ideological fanaticism accordingly gave way to political cynicism. In Poland, for example, some aspiring communist leaders of the new generation have made opportunistic appeals to nationalism, anti-Semitism, and anti-intellectualism in order to gain mass support. Labeled "the Partisans" because of their common wartime service in the small communist partisan movement, members of this group in recent times took control of the police and security apparatus. They take the position that Poland requires a more authoritarian regime and less interference from "liberal" intellectuals if the country's economic development is to be furthered. There is reason to believe that "the Partisans" have the sympathy of some of the new technocrats, eager to get on with the job of Polish economic development.

In a curious way, this emerging new Polish communist elite resembles the pre-World War II extreme right-wing groups in Poland more than it resembles either its Comintern-reared Stalinist predecessors or the earlier, internationalist founders of the Polish Communist Party. The program of the prewar rightists had typically included advocacy of a close alliance with Russia against Germany, the desirability of a homogeneous Polish state (and not one containing many minorities), a certain dose of anti-Semitism for mass consumption, violent emphasis on nationalism, and contempt for liberalism. Quite striking, and characteristic of the general decay of Marxism-Leninism, is the fact that many of the surviving prewar neofascist youth activists are now to be found among the most outspoken enthusiasts of the new Polish "communist" state—for the first time in centuries nationally homogeneous, allied with Russia against Germany, domestically authoritarian, and increasingly nationalist.* Similarly,

---

* Using nationalist demagogy, some members of this group also advocated, on the Rumanian model, somewhat less intense support for the Soviets, particularly on

one sees striking parallels between the ideology of the present Rumanian leadership and the prewar Iron Guard: modernization, industrialization, social revolution, nationalism. The labels have changed but the continuities suggest a political reincarnation.

Even independent Yugoslavia was not immune to the conflicting pulls resulting from the vague ideological preferences of the ruling elite and its power interests, from popular dissatisfaction and from intellectual desire for more freedom. The concerns of the elite pushed the political system toward more dictatorship and the maintenance of intimate ties with the communist world, while dissatisfaction among the people and intellectuals brought demands for closer relations with the West. Yugoslav internal policy zigzagged in response. Occasional measures of relaxation and decentralization, and a more permissive attitude toward contacts with the West, would be followed by periods of increased emphasis on party control, suppression of the intellectuals,[19] stimulation of closer relations with East Germany and the Soviet Union.

Such vacillation is likely to intensify after Tito's death. Because of his prestige and the loyalty he commands among the former partisans, Tito could absorb both the Eastern and the Western pulls without succumbing to either. His presence reassured the ruling elite that communist power was secure, even though Yugoslav independence dictated closer contacts with the West. Once he is gone, his successors for power are likely to split on the issue of relations with the East and the West. The party *apparatchiki*, likely to be supported by the Serbs and the more backward regions of Yugoslavia, might press for closer contacts with the East and for heavier industrial development within Yugoslavia, favoring the more backward regions. Spokesmen for the more developed parts of the country—Slovenia and Croatia—may insist on maintaining

the Sino-Soviet issues without, however, going to the other extreme of endorsing the Chinese. Such "separatism" was strongly opposed by Gomulka, who buttressed his ideological preference for Moscow also with open appeals to nationalism, including a special emphasis on the continued necessity of relying on Soviet support for the Oder-Neisse frontier.

the present, relatively decentralized system, with preferential treatment for the more developed regions and closer contacts with the West. Conflicting internal tendencies are likely to be aggravated by persisting nationality differences in the country, made even more serious by differences in levels of economic development.*

The resurgence of internal nationalist conflict also posed a threat to the stability of other East European states. In Czechoslovakia, the initially delayed process of de-Stalinization has already reawakened the perennial conflict between the Czechs and the Slovaks. The Slovak elite, which had suffered heavily under the Novotny-managed Stalinist purges, has been pressing for the rapid rehabilitation of the purged victims. In doing so, it has also stimulated a new wave of Slovak reactions against Prague control.

In Bulgaria, the purges which accompanied the Bulgarian-Yugoslav rapprochement indicated clearly that it had been opposed by significant elements in the Bulgarian party leadership. Zhivkov's opponents could, if the occasion arose, exploit this dramatic and popular issue and mobilize the anti-Yugoslav sentiments of the masses. The unfulfilled Bulgarian aspirations to Macedonia supply the potential source of mass nationalist support for alternative policies or alternative leadership. Such alternative leadership was available in the person of Vulko Chervenkov, a respected party leader replaced at the time of the Soviet-inspired turn toward Belgrade.

The revival of nationalism in East Europe thus has had a varied and far reaching impact on the politics of the region. Perhaps most important, by providing a sense of social cohesion and identity it created the basis for more effective resistance to Soviet domination. That opposition, moreover, reflected a development in the communist movement that Marx

---

* Secret negotiations with CEMA, conducted during the winter of 1963–64, and designed to establish Yugoslavia's "limited adhesion," (*L'Unità*, June 7, 1964) and which eventually culminated in Yugoslavia's "association" with CEMA, presumably reflected these conflicting pulls, especially since earlier Belgrade had sought—and then abandoned the effort—to obtain a peripheral association with EEC.

never anticipated: a regression from internationalism to nationalism in direct proportion to the passage of time since the communist revolution. The revolution was carried out by internationally oriented members of the intelligentsia. The Bolshevik leadership was international in outlook and even in national composition. The first postwar East European communist leaderships were composed of individuals who consciously subordinated their national identity to the "higher" cause of loyalty to the Soviet Union. But both in Russia (where Stalin massacred the "internationalists" and replaced them largely by a new generation of Russian peasant-stock *apparatchiki*) and in East Europe, where the Stalinists have gradually given way to a new elite, increasingly recruited from first generation proletarians, internationalism is now far weaker than among the corresponding elites in Western Europe, who by and large have "digested" their nationalism.

East European nationalism is not only and in every case directed against the Russians. Just as often its thrust points against a neighboring country, as for example in the cases of Hungary and Rumania (over the Transylvanian issue) or Yugoslavia and Bulgaria (over Macedonia). Nationalism not only inspires but also fragments East European opposition to the Russians, and helps the Soviet leaders in maintaining their predominance in the region by resorting to the ancient device of *divide et impera*. There is reason to believe that the Soviet leaders have encouraged Hungarian grievances over the handling of Hungarians in Transylvania as a way of putting pressure on Rumania and of solidifying its own relationship with Hungary. There is no doubt that the inability of the East Europeans to overcome their own national antipathies makes them much weaker in their efforts to reassert their independence.

Moreover, nationalism, as already suggested, is a divisive internal force in some of the multi-ethnic East European states. This is especially true of Yugoslavia and Czechoslovakia, but it applies also to the problem of minorities in Rumania and to a much lesser extent to the Hungarian minority in Slovakia. All such ethnic tensions serve to divide East Europe, to introduce bitter and often irrational conflicts, and to weaken the effectiveness of nationalism as a basis for opposition to Soviet domination.

The revival of nationalism does not necessarily foreshadow a more democratic internal development in the East European countries. The elites now taking over the somewhat more independent management of East European affairs are by and large composed of party bureaucrats, whose view of the world is a curious mixture of assertive nationalism (typical of the recently risen and politically awakened social groups) with some communist ideology, absorbed during their party training. Committed to vague notions of a just communist society and strongly believing in the advantages of industrialization, they tend to consider the state (and hence also their power positions) as the only instrument of social progress, and to couple their technocratic "statism" with increasing reliance on nationalism and better material conditions as a way of gaining popular support. Thus they differ profoundly from the 19th-century West European elites that promoted both the development and the democratization of their societies.

The societies they control, moreover, in most cases were devastated by the Nazis and in all cases drastically revolutionized by Stalinism. As a result, most of the middle class has been destroyed and there is still little social pluralism. Pressures from below require effective and democratic-minded leadership to become sources of democratization, and it is far from certain that the new industrial intelligentsia can provide it. In recent years, much of the humanistic and democratic criticism of the existing systems came from the revisionist intellectuals. But one may wonder whether they themselves are not already a phenomenon of the past, bound to disappear as the new industrial age replaces the traditional society. The libertarian, humanist intellectual (often associated with the café society of Warsaw or Budapest) is giving way to the functionally involved sociologists, planners, economists, etc. Neither they nor the industrial technocrats would for a minute sanction Stalinist terror, but many of them may be sympathetic to the idea that rapid social development requires a stable political order, more social discipline, and less intellectual dissent.

In the shorter run, therefore, the prospects for the democratization of East Europe seem somewhat dim. In the long run the attraction of a united Europe, the effects of closer contacts, and the opportunity to observe Western European welfare democracy will cumulatively tend to strengthen the process of social regeneration in East Europe and provide for wider public influence on decision making. In the meantime, the efforts of the rulers to strike a balance between communism and nationalism, between political constraints and freedom of expression result in ambiguous phases of relaxation and retrogression on the part of regimes that can no longer be described by a single label.

In analyzing East European internal trends, one should avoid replacing an old cliché with a new one. East Europe is no longer subject to "monolithic communism" but it is not dominated by pure and simple nationalism. Though it is no longer totalitarian in the Stalinist sense, it is not yet becoming democratic. Domination by the Soviet Union no longer automatically means internal terror, and independence of Soviet control does not necessarily involve internal liberalism. In fact, as noted already, in some cases new repressions have occurred. East Europe is now going through a period of technocratic-nationalist-communist dictatorships, and it should not be forgotten that the communist element still colors the perspectives of the ruling elites. The persistence of this influence is shown both in the dogmatism still affecting their internal policies and in the inclination, shared even by the Yugoslavs, to give the Soviet Union the benefit of the doubt on international issues. Eastern Europe is governed by an unsteady combination of nationalism and communism. The tensions between unity and diversity, between abstract dogmas and national peculiarities, and between the desire for democracy and the vested interests in bureaucratic dictatorships are the result.

The Implications of Russia's Europeanization

By the 1960's the Soviet posture on the world scene had become incongruous: a country with a powerful and modern industry and in some respects with an increasingly tolerable standard of social well-being,* was masquerading as the leader of the revolution of the globe's discontented, impoverished, and backward against the developed and the relatively wealthy. At home the Soviet communist elite justified its dictatorship by the argument that building communism was a universal historical process, which would not be completed merely by the construction of communism in the Soviet Union. Yet the increasing pressure of domestic needs made the Soviet leaders unwilling or unable to give the developing nations massive economic support, while the gradual bureaucratization of the Soviet elite and its sense of vested interest made it minimize the Soviet Union's active support for risky revolutionary ventures. The Sino-Soviet dispute revealed the increasing irrelevance of the Soviet Union to the revolutionary processes of our age, with the Soviet Union very gradually shifting from the role of an active supporter to that of a sympathetic spectator. The Chinese challenge made the Soviet leaders realize that the status quo was not quite as intolerable as their own proclamations had made it seem. The Cuban confrontation of 1962 dramatically revealed the limits of force in the nuclear age and led to the gradual decline in the attractiveness of the Soviet Union around the world among those who considered themselves to be revolutionaries.

The decay of the Soviet revolutionary identification was

---

* I.e., not just the individual's standard of consumption, which is still quite low by Western standards, but the total social benefits available to an individual in a relatively modern society: education, medical facilities, old age pensions, free vacations, social insurance, etc.

closely connected with the fragmentation of the Marxist-Leninist doctrine brought about by the gradual polarization of the Soviet and the Chinese positions. To Marxism, with its stress on the revolutionary role of the industrial proletariat in the capitalist society, Lenin had added the further element of the revolutionary "class alliance" between the proletariat and the peasantry, thereby making Marxism-Leninism relevant to conditions of political and economic underdevelopment (the precapitalist stage). The Soviet-Chinese dispute, with its respective charges of "ultrarevolutionary leftism" and "pacifist revisionism," gradually led the Chinese into an exaltation of peasant insurrections and the Soviets into making elaborate distinctions between "revolutions" which can even be peaceful and "the theory of violence" which is said to be both "militaristic" and "chauvinistic." [20] Perhaps even without quite realizing it, the Chinese, in a remarkable historical paradox, were emulating the precepts of the Russian Social Revolutionaries and the Soviets those of the Mensheviks, both early enemies of Leninism.

That Leninism, the specifically Russian contribution that transformed Marxism into a militant and totalitarian system, was now becoming the victim of the debate was clearly implied by Togliatti's last memorandum of the summer of 1964. In asking again what made Stalinism possible, he inevitably pointed to its antecedents. In demanding a polycentric international communist movement, he explicitly rejected the famous "21 conditions" that became the basis for the Comintern (praised again by Moscow a day after *Pravda* published Togliatti's views). In defending freedom for creative activity, he directly challenged the hallowed doctrine of "party-ness" (*partiinost*).* And just as earlier the criticism of Stalinism as an international system inevitably spread to a rejection of Stalinism as a form of domestic rule, it seemed likely that a reevaluation of Leninist norms for the international commu-

* Supremacy of the Party: subordination of all and everything to the will of the Party.

nist movement would eventually reopen the question of the
relevance of Leninism to domestic conditions vastly different
from those Lenin knew.

Already, the Soviet desire to gain the support of other
communist parties against the Chinese has forced the Soviet
leaders to compromise their past position as the authoritative
interpreters of Marxism-Leninism. They could no longer afford
to insist that their interpretation, including the somewhat grad-
ualist formulations adopted in the course of the Sino-Soviet
dispute, were binding on all parties. Instead, the Soviet leaders
were stressing that there is no "general line," that all parties
can "creatively" interpret the doctrine, that specific conditions
can dictate particular emphases and adjustments. A formerly
absolutist and universal ideology was thus becoming relativ-
ized and particularized. The resulting dilemma had been posed
earlier by Ulbricht when he plaintively asked, "Who is the one
who determines what is truth, and what complies with the
principles of the Marxist-Leninist doctrine?"

The destruction of communist universalism was accompanied by an internal communist refutation of the alleged
"iron laws" of historical development. The Chinese leaders
charged that the Soviet Union was engaged in the extensive
restoration of capitalism. Thus history, which has been said by
communists to move immutably from feudalism to capitalism
to socialism to communism was now, according to the Chinese
communists, inexplicably reversing itself, from socialism back
to . . . capitalism! The Soviet leaders, who had for years been
proving the inevitability of their ultimate victory by citing the
expansion of the communist camp from one country to one
billion people, were instead informing their adherents that two-
thirds of that camp was in the hands of "petty bourgeois
nationalist neo-Trotskyites." Both leaderships lamely attempted to explain how this could have happened, but their
explanations really added up to the proposition that a process
supposedly subject to historical inevitability had been subordinated to unpredictable historical contingency.

Both leaderships indicated they recognized and were troubled by their inability to account for this development. In Suslov's words to the Central Committee (February 14, 1964): "Everyone inevitably asks himself the question: 'How could it happen that the leaders of such a party as the CCP, [Communist Party of China] which has behind it considerable experience in revolutionary struggle and building a new society, have taken the road of struggle against the worldwide communist movement?' " Together with the relativization of the previously absolute principles and the decline in their universal applicability, the subordination of historical inevitability to unpredictable historical contingency added up to nothing less than the accelerating erosion of Marxism-Leninism as a vital force. In form, the struggle with the Chinese was over the corpse of Stalinism; in effect, the chief victim was Marxism-Leninism.

The debate with China had another important effect on the Soviet Union, especially relevant for the West: it tended to push Russia into Europe. The Soviet leaders and their supporters have repeatedly complained about the "sinification" of Marxism-Leninism,* and this charge was not without justification. Disappointed with the Soviets, the Chinese leaders developed a theory of the historical "shift in the center of gravity" of the world revolution from west to east: from France to Germany, from Germany to Russia, and finally from Russia to Asia. China was said to be the "center of gravity" of the world revolution and the developed world increasingly the revolution's enemy.[21] A natural corollary was the Chinese effort to identify the USSR as a European power; Moscow was intensely outraged by the public Chinese efforts to expel the USSR from the various procommunist Afro-Asian organizations. At the

---

* "Chinese propaganda openly maintains that Mao Tse-tung's ideas are a higher incarnation of Marxism-Leninism; that our era is the era of Mao Tse-tung and that his teaching is the most correct and most complete Marxism-Leninism of the contemporary period." Speech by Secretary Andropov on the occasion of Lenin's birth anniversary, April 22, 1964. See also B. Bogunovic, "The Sinification of Marxism," *Politika,* (Belgrade) May 1, 2, and 3, 1964.

same time, Peking spokesmen stressed the enormous significance of the Chinese contribution to world culture and to the spread of civilization.

The Soviet reaction was symptomatic. While vigorously protesting its credentials as a Euro-Asian power and hence entitled to participation in Afro-Asian organizations, the Soviet spokesmen gradually began to take up the cudgels in the defense of Europe against the Chinese or Asian menace. An absurd debate developed between Soviet and Chinese historians, writing in academic journals, as to who first discovered America: the European Columbus or the Chinese Huei Shen, with the Soviet scholars finally condescendingly observing that "it is quite possible that Huei Shen was accidentally carried by a storm to the shores of America, but this had no social significance whatsoever. . . ." [22] Somewhat more serious was the debate over the historical function of the Mongol invasions. The Chinese claimed that the invasions had contributed to European cultural development by bringing Europe in contact with China, and in this connection they glorified Genghis Khan as a great hero; the Soviets emphasized the calamities brought upon Europe by these invasions and wondered how the Chinese "philosophy, literature and art" could have been studied in "the ashes of cities and towns destroyed by the Mongol hordes." * Denying further that the leading European thinkers, "from Descartes to Hegel," had been influenced by Confucian thought, the Soviet historians deplored the Chinese inclination toward "defamation in every possible way of everything 'European.' "

Doubtless, the Soviet reaction was also stimulated by the rising Chinese threat to the Soviet eastern frontiers, imposed on China by imperial Russia. Taken together, the political attacks on Chinese leadership, the scornful comments about

---

* An even more vigorous attack was made by Bulgarian historians who argued that Genghis Khan had engaged in genocide but that fortunately in the end the Mongol hordes were stopped "at the threshold of Czechoslovakia" [sic!] See V. Sokolov and A. Mironov, "Serving Nationalist Aspirations—On Certain Concepts of Contemporary Chinese Historians," *Narodna Armiya*, April 30, 1964.

Chinese social and economic backwardness, and the wide-spread practice of Soviet politicians, diplomats, journalists, and scholars of stressing in their private conversations with Westerners the "Asiatic character" of the Chinese, this "defense" of Europe reflected a significant change in the Russian attitude. The Sino-Soviet dispute thus not only fragmented the former bloc and its ideology; China, by posing a direct challenge to Russia, including the touchy issue of Soviet frontiers in the east, was prompting an emerging sense of identification with Europe—a "Europeanization" of Russia—even to the point of usurpation by Russians of the old Polish and German claim to being the eastern borderland of the threatened Western civilization.

If it turns out that the Sino-Soviet dispute has precipitated the gradual divorce of the Soviet Union from active participation in the revolutionary movement of the second half of this century, the Soviet internal development can be seen as having created the necessary preconditions. It permitted the Soviet leaders—in this case, strongly supported by their people—to consider other options than those advocated by the Chinese and to make a choice with their own actual material—as well as political—interests in mind. By itself economic change might not have had so direct a political effect. But the shock effect of the Sino-Soviet dispute caused a shift in the elite's perspectives and this also meant a shift in the nature of domestic Soviet power. The ruling *apparatchiki*, increasingly dominated by small-town and rural elements who had risen to power in the 1930's and 1940's, their outlook characterized by tough-minded nationalism and simple-minded dogmatism,[23] were neither interested in risking their positions on behalf of dangerous revolutionary ventures, nor in promoting a liberal democracy in the Soviet Union. Thus they turned to massive indoctrination as a means of counteracting the increasing susceptibility of the Soviet people, especially the intelligentsia, to Western influence [24] and to great power nationalism as a means of legitimizing power. In some ways, their behavior was reminiscent of the earlier periods of American or German chauvinism. The immodest stress on national achievements and on Soviet primacy as a great power, while certainly not absent in the past, became more and more the main link between the people and the rulers, and the dominant motif in the Soviet outlook.

Great-power nationalism can be very assertive and tenacious. Therefore, it would be premature to expect a precipitous decline in the intensity of Soviet-American tensions because of the domestic changes. The competition between these two superpowers will continue because both continue to have, however vaguely defined, a global sense of mission and both remain the world's principal military powers. Conflicts of interest between them are inescapable. But both the nature of the conflict and its geographic focus may change with the evolution of Soviet society and national orientation. Europe could become an area where both sides see an advantage in obtaining stability, even while waging political warfare elsewhere.

Soviet behavior on the world scene seemed in keeping with the above trend. Soviet international prestige rose in inverse proportion to the ideological faithfulness of Soviet policies. Noticing it, Khrushchev and the other Soviet leaders increasingly acted as if they confined international communism, with its revolutionary obligations, to the dustbin of history (to use one of their own favorite expressions), and as if they wished to replace it by a loosely linked "International Dictatorships, Inc." The courtship of Ben Bella, Nkrumah, Sukarno, or Nasser, essentially nationalist leaders, and Nasser then still notorious for his suppression of communists, the ostentatious references to Ben Bella and Nasser as "comrades" and to their policies as "building socialism" were, it seems, more than just a tactical maneuver. Rather, they constituted an effort to forge an ideologically diffuse international system, based on a common hostility to the United States and/or "Western imperialists," and led by the USSR. The revolutionary quality of the new constellation would be more external than internal; i.e., it would be against the international status quo, but not necessarily for internal communization. Even if one makes allowances for the Soviet long-range hope that eventually these national dictatorships will become communist, the new constellation was far removed from the old communist camp, led by the USSR in its capacity as the first communist state and composed of "monolithically united" communist states. Within this community there was still an inner core of "like-minded communist states" which were tied together by the power interests of the ruling elites and by their broadly generalized ideological preferences, ranging in content from the revisionist Tito to the Stalinist Ulbricht; but even for these, the Soviet wooing of Nasser, as well as the Soviet inability to cope with Rumania, was bound to prove infectious.*

The gradual decline of the ideological factor in international politics contributed to the further reassertion of the primacy of statehood in East Europe. Both the Yugoslav and the Rumanian cooperation with the United States signaled this change. It was even more dramatically illustrated by the limited areas of Soviet-American cooperation, and by the Chinese communist speculation about a new "second intermediate zone" in international politics, to be composed of France, West Germany, England, and Japan, and to be aimed,

---

* *Polityka,* (Warsaw), October 3, 1964, carries a long letter refuting the views of a reader who argued that if Algeria is considered a "socialist" state, and yet it has Islam as its state religion, then Poland can be a "socialist" state with Catholicism as its official religion. For example, the reader first cited the "official" view on Algeria and Islam and then in a parallel column he adapted it to the Polish conditions:

"The Algerian nation is deeply attached to Islam. Islam is not only a religion, but also a form of national culture, a tradition, a custom. In the era of colonialism, Islam constituted the most important factor of ideological resistance, of the maintenance of national and cultural individuality."

"The Polish nation is deeply attached to its religion. Catholicism is not only a religion, but, even more, a form of national culture, a tradition and a custom. In the period of the rule of the partitioning powers, Catholicism constituted one of the most important factors of resistance against germanization and russification, a factor in the maintenance of national and cultural individuality."

in cooperation with China, against the two superpowers.[25] This conception pitted four "capitalist" powers together with China, against the two superpowers, both charged with the desire of establishing a joint hegemony over the world, irrespective of the profound differences in their respective social systems. The Chinese conception made a mockery of ideologically-founded alliances, while the Sino-Soviet border incidents meant that the possibility of limited armed clashes between communist states could no longer be excluded. These precedents were now part of history and their significance could not be erased by the post-Khrushchev effort to contain the Sino-Soviet split.

The change meant a further decline in the reliance on absolutist ideological legitimation for the existence of the Soviet bloc in Europe (formerly presented as part of the inevitable transformation of humanity into socialism-communism), and the increased importance of more pragmatic, transitional, and national-interest considerations in keeping the Soviet Euro-Asian community together. For example, in the case of Poland and Czechoslovakia, the ties of their elites to the Soviet Union were reinforced by national fears of a resurgent Germany. In both Poland and Czechoslovakia there was an overwhelming consensus that they could not afford to face Germany alone, given the uncertainty of the German long-range eastern goals. The Polish and Czech attitudes immeasurably contributed to the containment of centrifugal forces within the Soviet areas of predominance.* This is less true of the Balkans, where such national-interest ties with the Soviet Union are less self-evident, apart from the appeal of the anti-German line in Yugoslavia. There is little to bind Ru-

---

* Their collective interest in "defending" East Germany against the West justified the Soviet military presence not only in Germany but also in Poland. Although there is no necessary connection between loyalty to Moscow and Soviet military presence (as shown by Czechoslovakia, which has been loyal without Soviet occupation forces), nonetheless it is a fact that no defiance of Moscow has successfully taken place where there have been Soviet troops—and there have been no Soviet troops where defiance has been successful (Yugoslavia, Albania, China, North Vietnam, North Korea, Rumania).

mania or Bulgaria to the Soviet Union, and hence the Soviet leadership will be increasingly compelled to demonstrate the "objective" benefits of alliance. This will mean increased stress on economic assistance, especially as the ideological identification slowly declines in importance.

The greater viability and reliability of ties based on such national-interest considerations may eventually prompt the Soviet leadership to a drastic reevaluation of its position in Europe. Such a revision will become more likely as Soviet internal evolution and the Sino-Soviet conflict create greater receptivity to change. In retrospect, it is remarkable how quickly the Soviet domination of East Europe has been undermined: in 1945 the Soviet Union enjoyed military predominance over the region; by 1948 it had also consolidated its political predominance, in the process gaining Czechoslovakia but losing Yugoslavia; and by 1953 it had fully subordinated all the ruling elites, imposed a uniform pattern of ideological orthodoxy and widespread economic exploitation; but by 1956 the political, ideological, and economic hegemony had been gravely weakened and by 1964 two more East European countries had defied Moscow overtly and the Soviet capacity to direct the others was largely neutralized by the Chinese option.

In East Europe of the sixties the historical pull is westward; to paraphrase Mao Tse-tung, "The West wind prevails over the East wind." The East Europeans now increasingly think of links with West Europe and the Russians look east with growing apprehension. Given the recent pace of events, one can only speculate about the shape of Soviet-East European relations by 1970 or 1975. Out of inertia and out of a fading commitment to the revolutionary mystique, the Soviet Union is likely to try to hang on to Eastern Europe. It may do so even while competing with the United States elsewhere and even while faced with increased Chinese pressure. Nevertheless, the domestic evolution of the Soviet society, especially as accelerated under the impact of the Sino-Soviet dispute, creates the grounds for an eventual acceptance by the Soviets of a European settlement. The more rapidly growing interest of the East Europeans in such a settlement may at best influence the Russians to accept it. At the very least, it will create fissures in the Soviet relationship with East Europe. It is no longer beyond the realm of possibility that in the course of the next decade or so the Soviet leaders will reluctantly conclude that their position in East Europe would be stronger if the East European states ceased to be unpopular and unstable dictatorships, and instead came to resemble Finland. They might conclude that only a politically stable East Europe—and not one dominated by insecure communist power elites, subscribing to an eroding doctrine and thrashing around for a substitute in nationalism—can effectively serve the interests of Soviet security.

CHAPTER TWO

Dismantling the
Iron Curtain

The European partition is very slowly being undone in the cultural and economic realms. Step by step, closer links between Western and Eastern Europe are being forged, although the process has been meeting with some resistance from both sides. Broadly speaking, the East European governments favor dismantling the Iron Curtain rapidly in the economic field while lifting it only very gradually in the social. The Western countries plead for the elimination of cultural restraints but are somewhat more ambivalent on the subject of economic relations. At the same time, the intensive industrialization of Eastern Europe is making the earlier economic backwardness of the region a thing of the past. East Europe, in spite of its present economic difficulties, no longer needs to fear that a return to Europe would also mean a reversion to its former status as Europe's backyard. However, for the ruling communist elites the relatively uniform rate of both West and East European industrial development is posing a mounting ideological challenge.

"Against Ideological Coexistence"

Ten years after Stalin's death East Europe, with the exception of Albania, was already reasonably accessible to outsiders and the Western visitor was no longer an uncommon sight. Visa restrictions have been largely modified and in some cases, such as for brief trips from Austria to Hungary and

Czechoslovakia, visas are no longer a formal requirement. In the summer of 1964, the Rumanian government announced that Western tourists could obtain Rumanian visas on arrival at Rumanian border posts, including airports, and the Hungarian government shortly after followed suit. It could now even be said that travel to a "People's Democracy" is easier from the West than from another "People's Democracy." Cultural exchange agreements with Western countries have also restored some contact between the East European intellectual community and the West. Jamming of Western radio programs is no longer practiced throughout the entire area; VOA and BBC get through to most East European countries and to Russia, and by 1964 even Radio Free Europe was no longer jammed in Hungary and Rumania, although jamming continued by the Czechs, the Bulgarians, and the Russians (who jammed RFE broadcasts to Poland).

It would be inaccurate, however, to foster the impression that by the mid-sixties East Europe had broken out from the isolation imposed upon it during the Stalinist late forties. A closer look at the contacts that have so far developed reveals that they are still relatively limited both in scope and in form. Most cultural contacts are still subject to formal arrangements and, therefore, official control. Cultural contacts have usually been governed by formal or semiformal annual (in some cases, two-year) agreements either between the governments concerned or between the governments and delegated institutions, such as the British Council or some of the American foundations. The British Council has been most active in Yugoslavia and Poland, while Foreign Office protocols have governed British arrangements with the other communist states. In the French Foreign Ministry, the Bureau of East-West Exchanges of the General Directory of Cultural and Technical Affairs has negotiated the relevant protocols for cultural exchanges for France with all East European states, even including Albania. Such intergovernmental arrangements do not exclude other bilateral relations between institutes, such as for instance the twinning up of the universities of Yale and Kiev or Göttingen and Poznan, or exchanges of visits between various specialized institutions and organizations. Typically, however, such specific relationships are provided for in the intergovernmental arrangements and, in any case, are subject to the communist country's Ministry of Higher Education or Foreign Affairs.

The application of this general pattern differs in its specifics from country to country.[1] On the Eastern side, Poland, Hungary, and above all Yugoslavia have been the most responsive to the Western desire for closer contact. On the Western European side, the lead has been taken by England, France, and Germany. In recent times Italy has also become involved, especially in the Balkans.* France has been most active in Poland and the Soviet Union, where French professors and lecturers teach in some of the leading institutions. West Germany has succeeded in establishing extensive contacts, particularly with Czechoslovakia,† but also with Poland and, to a lesser extent, with the other East European states, without having formal cultural agreements with them—or even, perhaps, *because* there were no such agreements. The East European governments have been unwilling to negotiate formal agreements with West Germany in view of the West German insistence that West Berlin be covered by them. Yet the new atmosphere created by de-Stalinization and the energetic initiatives by private or semiprivate German institutions have resulted in the development of a very active program of exchanges and visits.[2]

In evaluating the development of East-West European cultural relations, it is important to preserve a sense of balance. Though there is certainly an improvement over the earlier condition of almost no contacts at all, cultural, scientific, and artistic contacts are still relatively meager. The cultural exchanges between the West European and the East European

---

* The Italians have been especially active in Rumania, and the Rumanians, anxious to emphasize their Latin ties, have been quite responsive.

† Typical, for example, was a 45-hour series on German TV about Czechoslovakia, prepared jointly in 1964 by the Germans and the Czechs.

states and the Soviet Union involve individuals or groups of individuals; five professors here, ten or twenty graduate students there, a formal conference of journalists, a delegation of health experts, an opera tour, and so on. To cite several examples, the 1963–64 British arrangement with Hungary, Czechoslovakia, Rumania, and Bulgaria called for the exchange of two postgraduate scholars for each of the countries involved, to be increased in 1964–65 in the Czech and Hungarian cases to four each. The number of Soviet postgraduate students in the United Kingdom during 1963–64 was 19. Of the 1,057 French personnel teaching French throughout Europe, only 48 were in East Europe and Russia (the largest number, 14, in Yugoslavia).

The situation is even more undesirable with respect to the written word. It seems that the communist leaders are most fearful of it; perhaps this is because of memories of their own proselytization in which the printed word played such an important role. There is still no free circulation of Western press in Eastern Europe and the Soviet Union, with the exception of Yugoslavia. Some Western newspapers are occasionally available in the capitals on the newsstands in the hotels frequented by foreigners.* Western newspapers mailed to individuals other than officials are not delivered in most cases. While foreign books are sold in large numbers, they are subject to official selection and any containing "unorthodox" political or ideological views are excluded.† Efforts to arrange open and unrestricted sales of British books in Russia met with repeated rebuffs. At British insistence, the Anglo-Soviet agree-

---

* By 1964, Poland and Czechoslovakia had concluded formal arrangements for the sale of Western publications, but the agreements stipulate that they are available for foreign visitors. While visiting Prague and Bucharest during September 1964, the writer was unable to obtain any Western non-communist press. The number of copies imported for sale to Western tourists is ridiculously low: for example, Poland and Czechoslovakia import no more than about 300 copies of *The New York Times* and about 150 copies of *Le Monde*.

† Of the 82 million copies of periodicals and newspapers exported by France only 2,044,000 went to East Europe and the Soviet Union; of the 89,624,000 books, only 2,618,000 (Poland taking one half of the books).

ment had provided for the exchange of librarians and pub-
lishers. This item in practice was simply ignored by the Soviet
side.

The obstacles to a free and open exchange appear to be
rooted in a strongly-held communist view that "ideological
coexistence" is by definition counterrevolutionary. Khrushchev
said as much in his March 8, 1963, speech: "Let us analyze
what would happen to Soviet art if the proponents of peaceful
coexistence between different ideological tendencies had their
way with literature and art. In the first place, a blow would
have been struck at our revolutionary conquests and socialist
art. According to the logic of the struggle, things would not
stop there. There is no certainty but that these people having
regained strength *would try to attack the achievements of the
Revolution*" (italics added). Insufficiently critical accounts of
life in France and the United States led Khrushchev in the
same speech to observe that: "It sometimes happens that the
journeys of our writers in foreign countries, far from being
useful, turn out to be against our country. . . ."

Khrushchev's attitude is shared by many *apparatchiki* in
the now more independent East European dictatorships. Indeed, as already noted, independence often accentuates the
fears of the elites. In Poland, the Fourth Party Congress held
in June 1964 heard extensive warnings from a rapidly rising
younger leader, R. Strzelecki, reputed to be the head of the
"Partisans" (see Chapter I, page 32), against the new Western
policy of "softening" the East European states.[3] A more extensive analysis of this alleged Western policy was presented in a
lecture to the Political Academy of the Hungarian Communist
Party by Dezso Nemes, a Politburo member and a Central Committee Secretary. As he put it, "The 'relaxing' propaganda of the
Western powers turns with special attention toward the intelligentsia. They regard the engineers, doctors, scientists, artists,
teachers, writers and other representatives of cultural life, who
are trying to keep away from the ideological and political
struggle, as easily impressionable subjects. The broadening of

cultural relations, as well as the development of tourism, do, in fact, increase the possibility of Western ideological and moral penetration." [4]

These fears explain why cultural contacts with the communist states have not been developing spontaneously but are still subject to official controls. There is still no such thing as a free flow of ideas and intellectuals between Eastern and Western Europe, although the situation has been improving, and the pressures on its behalf from East European intellectuals have been rising.* Nemes, in his militant speech, rejected any notion of a return to a policy of complete isolation, pointing out that "it would represent a retreat in the ideological struggle which, during the course of the peaceful coexistence of the two world systems, we cannot avoid pursuing." The communist rulers would prefer to impose maximum controls over such contacts,† and to channel them primarily from the standpoint of their own specific educational, technological, or economic needs.

Characteristically, the communist governments are especially responsive to independent initiatives from Western firms which enable technicians from communist states to become acquainted with Western technology and knowhow,‡ with the consequent danger of at least a partial imposition on the West of a pattern of exchange preferred by the other side. Similarly, unless the West is extremely selective in the criteria guiding the award of Western fellowships, there is the possibility of an ominous paradox: Western fellowships, eagerly sought by the East European, could become part of an award system for

---

* See, for example, the outspoken demand for more contacts with the West by R. Selucky, "We and the World," *Literarni Noviny*, September 5, 1964.
† Disagreement over the extent of these controls led in 1962 to the Ford Foundation's suspension of its exchange program with Poland, pursued with great success since 1957, and to abortive efforts on the part of some Polish communist officials to prevent the implementation of such a program with Hungary (which the Foundation arranged in the summer of 1964).
‡ For example, of the 1,800 Russians with commercial or technical competence who visited the United Kingdom in 1962–63, only 300 came under the exchange agreement.

regime loyalists. To attain that end, the East European governments have attempted to gain control over the nominations for fellowships provided by Western governments or by such American institutions as the Ford Foundation.

A broader aspect of East-West contacts involves the growth of tourism. At the present time, relatively few West Europeans visit the East. The idea that East Europe is inaccessible has become a habit of thought with many Westerners and under any circumstances it would be difficult for East Europe to compete with Spain, Italy, France, or Greece, either in tourist attractions or in the facilities and conveniences that are nowadays required. Moreover the average Western tourist objects to the unavailability of Western press, the obligation in the Soviet case to abide by advance itineraries and geographic off-limits zones, the cumbersome procedures governing currency exchange, and other restrictive regulations still applied in these countries.

Tables I and II in the Appendix compare several Western and Eastern European nations in terms of the number of their citizens who have traveled to the countries listed and in terms of the total number of foreign visitors to each. While it would be inaccurate to ascribe the differences only to political considerations, since East Europe has not been traditionally an area of international tourism and East Europeans before World War II traveled abroad less than the West Europeans, the disparity does reinforce the persisting sense of isolation from the mainstream of European life. The contrast with Franco's authoritarian and restrictive Spain speaks for itself: more than three times as many Spaniards traveled abroad as Poles, even though the populations of the two countries are approximately even. The comparison is even more unfavorable to East Europe if some crude matching is done of countries roughly comparable in terms of their geographic location, climate, and size: for example, the Austrian total is more than four times that of adjoining Hungary, which by 1964 had become the most accessible communist country; the West

German over 15 times that for Poland and Czechoslovakia combined. The only exception is Yugoslavia, which had opened its frontiers already in the very early fifties. The majority of foreign visitors to East Europe and the Soviet Union come from within the communist world, ranging from one-half in the Soviet case to approximately three-fourths for the East European states, the only marked exception again being Yugoslavia. Yet even with respect to this internal bloc travel, East Europe remains remarkably parochial: little effort has been made to develop large-scale mobility, and there is simply no parallel to the organized Franco-German efforts to arrange for exchanges of young people (it is estimated that in 1964 some 250,000 will be involved).[5] This restricted mobility in East Europe has had negative economic implications. Whereas labor has moved relatively freely in West Europe, in East Europe Czechoslovakia has suffered from a labor shortage both in industry and in agriculture, which even forced some plants to close and required a revision of the 1961–65 plan,[6] while neighboring Poland has acknowledged it suffers from mounting unemployment.[7]

The number of East Europeans traveling westward is considerably smaller than the number of East Europeans who travel to other communist states. Restrictions on travel to the West are primarily political in origin, but currency exchange difficulties contribute to this condition and make it easier for the ruling elites to impose restraints on such travel.* Further-

* According to the report prepared by the Central and Eastern European Commission of the European Movement (mimeographed, 1963), p. 27: "A prospective Polish or Hungarian traveler to the West must satisfy the following requirements: a) produce a written invitation issued by a relative or a friend in the West, countersigned by a local consular officer; b) obtain an entry permit (or visa) to the country concerned, based on the same invitation and assurance of full support during the visit; c) produce evidence that no obligations as regards his work or other duties would be neglected as a result of his trip; d) apply to the District Passport Office usually attached to the District Police Headquarters for the issue of the passport (which normally entitles the traveler to visit all the countries of Europe and/or other parts of the world for a period not longer than two years). . . . According to general practice, no families are allowed to leave the country together—a wife, or a child being left as 'hostage' against the possibility of the traveler's defection." (This latter restriction is now less rigidly enforced.)

more, strict Western requirements for passports and visas also inhibit East-West travel.* There is no doubt that the East European youth would take advantage of any opening of the frontiers; the desire to see the West is one of the constantly voiced aspirations of the younger generation. But the restrictions make for a marked disparity in the extent to which East Europeans participate in the annual "European migration" that has gained such momentum since the war and which, as West European public opinion polls suggest, contributes significantly to the formation of a "European" mentality.†

Nonetheless, there has been a steady increase in the volume of East-West travel. Preliminary figures for 1964 showed that travel to Yugoslavia from the East had grown considerably and that many more Hungarians had traveled westward. There was also a growing official interest in attracting more Western tourists to East Europe if only to provide hard currency. The growth in travel, in its turn, has provoked further expressions of concern by some of the ruling *apparatchiki,* thereby providing additional evidence that the West continues to attract the East, and that the attraction is great enough to be regarded as a threat by the ruling elites.‡

* The Danish government, however, waived this requirement in 1964.

† See *Sondages,* No. 1, 1963, for European attitudes of the travelers and non-travelers, and A. Lijphart, "Tourist Traffic and Integration Potential," *Journal of Common Market Studies,* February 1964, for a more analytical discussion. Also, *ibid.,* November 1963, p. 125, for fuller data from Gallup International on impact of travel on "European" attitudes.

Of the more than five million visitors to Austria in 1962, only 17,223 came from neighboring Hungary, 9,389 from neighboring Czechoslovakia, 1,984 from Bulgaria, 10,489 from Poland, and 2,790 from the Soviet Union. While approximately 2 million came to the United Kingdom in 1963, the visas issued to visitors from the Soviet Union numbered only 3,020; from Czechoslovakia, 2,279; from Hungary, 4,915; from Poland, 7,319; from Bulgaria, 434; and from Rumania, 527. (Similar data could be cited for other states.) What is even more striking is the small number of visitors from the East European states to Yugoslavia: of the total 1,240,000 in 1962, only 5,728 were from Czechoslovakia, 17,743 from East Germany, 21,620 from Poland, 5,699 and 2,424 from neighboring Bulgaria and Rumania respectively, 10,436 from the USSR; in contrast, for example, to 304,984 Austrians, 262,957 West Germans, 78,947 from the United Kingdom, and 38,886 from the Netherlands.

‡ For Czech fears of the ideological impact of tourism, see, for example, L. Manousek, "Some Problems of the Ideological Work of the Party in the South

"For Economic Coexistence"

If the communist governments can be said to fear "ideological peaceful coexistence," they certainly seem fearless in preaching "economic peaceful coexistence." In fact, their unwillingness to revert to the self-imposed isolation of the past was closely related, as the Hungarian Politburo member Nemes admitted, to the desire of the communist states to develop more extensive economic relations with the West, even though, in his view, "the gangster character of imperialism remains the same." [8] Pleas for increased trade relations, including when-

---

Moravian Region," *Rovnost*, April 9, 1964, in which the author expresses concern for "the socialist consciousness" of the people because of the influence of foreign tourists.

For a more general statement reflecting the fears of the local *apparatchiki*, see J. Smetana, *Nova Svoboda*, May 5, 1964 (both Smetana and Manousek write for small regional papers), from which a lengthy and revealing passage deserves citation:

"Some people interpret our efforts to bring about better relations with the Western countries in a curious way. They are always ready to show to the visitors from West Germany, England and France how overwhelmed they are by admiration for their civilization, forgetting their own pride and the fact that society cannot be judged by individuals, or by the fact that they have more striking things, say, fountain pens, than those we can buy in our shops.

Capitalism has not remained stationary, it keeps advancing. We have discarded the old dogmas on this point, and there are people who immediately go a step further and would almost present to us the capitalist countries as a shining example and say that all people there live better than we do in this country, overlooking the fact that the capitalist world is unequally developed and that we, too, are still busy overcoming its heritage, that hundreds of thousands of people in some African, Asian and South American countries sweat and slave for the main capitalist countries.

Unfortunately, of late part of our press has also contributed to this, with the appearance of a flood of articles about the capitalist countries in it, in which one-sided experiences are described and which are full of compliments for the gilding.

When literati from the West come to us, they are immediately told that they should write and say what they want, that everything will be published, even if what they said was contrary to the principles of our life and of our Party. Polemics with them—but where!

Of late, our economy has been much discussed. We are also looking for ways of our own, somewhat different from those of the Soviet economy. We are like pupils who have already learned so much from their teacher that they can better learn to work according to their own conditions. At once there are people who add various remarks to this meritorious and by no means easy activity, to the effect *how far we could have been long ago, had we had some kind of economy of our own from the beginning"* (italics added).

ever possible long-term Western credits, have been repeated by the top Soviet and East European leaders to every important Western visitor, by the leading communist economists and journals, by Khrushchev in the course of his visits to Western Europe and the United States, and by Brezhnev, in his very first major address on November 6, 1964. The Soviet leaders, who in 1958 condemned Poland and Yugoslavia for taking U.S. credits, were now looking the other way when even orthodox Czechoslovakia hinted publicly that it would welcome them.* Thus closer economic contacts with the West were presumably no longer objectionable *per se* and acceptance of Western aid was no longer tantamount to defiance of the USSR. This development also implies, of course, that such closer contacts were no longer necessarily and in every case a political gain for the West. Nonetheless, close economic ties with the West might still be objectionable to the Soviet leaders if they followed or were accompanied by political changes in the relations with the Soviet Union—as in the Rumanian case.

The desire for trade and Western credits was most often justified by communist spokesmen on the grounds that it would contribute to peace. Perhaps so, but in fact even more important were the inability of the communist economies to meet rising consumer demands without an expansion of trade with the industrially advanced Western countries and the increasingly widespread realization that internal investment needs are not likely to be met within the framework of CEMA.

A further reason for the drive for Western trade and credits is the need of the communist economies for Western specialized equipment and knowhow, particularly in the more sophisticated and recent branches of industry, such as chemicals, plastics, rayons, all of which have consumer applica-

* Symptomatic of the general communist interest in this and the Soviet approval were the Czech comments to the effect that extensive Western loans to Yugoslavia and Yugoslav production under Western licenses were not incompatible with building socialism. (Radio Prague, June 1, 1964.) In his June 3, 1958, speech in Sofia and the July 11, 1958, in East Berlin, Khrushchev had ridiculed Yugoslav socialism as the kind built on American alms.

tion. The earlier industrial drives had stressed the development of the more traditional branches of heavy industry (steel became a particularly important status symbol), and by the sixties the Soviet and the East European leaders found that they had neglected to keep up with the development of many novel branches of industrial production. Several of the communist states, such as Poland, were also faced with an acute investment problem intensified by rapid population growth and mounting unemployment. The Poles even had to resort to keeping down the level of worker productivity both in industry and agriculture,* thereby perpetuating an unhealthy economic condition.

By the sixties it was clear that CEMA was not capable of providing an adequate solution. Its late start, combined with the after-effects of the Stalinist policy of promoting industrial autarky in each communist state, had worked against it.[9] To some states, such as Rumania, CEMA's later remedy, the specialization and division of labor, propounded by Khrushchev, seemed to strike at the very heart of their own national ambitions. Furthermore, tighter integration in CEMA, even if holding out some economic advantages, could eventually serve to limit national independence and could become a powerful control lever in the hands of the Soviet leaders.

Credits were also important to the Russians because of their balance-of-payments problems. The Soviets and East Europeans need credits in part because they would otherwise have to pay with hard currency for some of their activities in the developed parts of the world, for their assistance to Cuba, particularly in leasing shipping, not to mention also their global subversive operations. That this consideration should not be underrated is suggested by the fact that even a country as wealthy as America has had some second thoughts with

---

* For example, employment in the Polish textile industry was to rise even though the industry was capable of reducing it while increasing production. This problem is discussed in a comparative evaluation of the Polish and Czech economies in *Rude Pravo*, June 27, 1964.

respect to its military posture in Germany and elsewhere because of its own balance-of-payments problems. It is likely that the Russians have encountered comparable difficulties with regard to their political obligations and activities.*

This need for trade and credits explains the very agitated tone of communist comments on the Common Market. Communist spokesmen have shown great alarm at the dangers of discrimination against them by this group.† They have objected vigorously not only to the higher tariffs imposed on imports from outside the Common Market countries, but also to the declining role of bilateral trade agreements with countries outside the Common Market, seeing in this a marked decrease in their room for economic maneuver.

The communists have also stressed their opposition to the embargo imposed by the West, chiefly the United States, on exports of "strategic" goods to the East. In recent years the West Europeans have succeeded in whittling down the list to items of essentially direct military application, though the American list still includes such indirectly military items as chemical plants and oil refineries, so that the embargo affects only to a very limited extent the general volume of East-West trade.[10] The communists are nonetheless most insistent in their attacks on it.

The cumulative effect of the overt economic needs for trade with the West and of the more implicit political fears of Soviet-sponsored economic integration has been a considerable increase in East-West trade. In the decade from 1955 (when the desire for Western trade "surfaced" in the East and be-

---

* NATO estimates put at about $200-300 million annually the cost of Soviet foreign propaganda and external political activity. (*The New York Times,* September 16, 1964.)

† Typical was a statement by a Polish economic journal in August 1963: "A common commercial policy of the Common Market countries creates the possibility of a simultaneous stopping of imports or exports by all six member countries. Let us simply recall the embargo in the recent period of the cold war to realize the full danger contained in this intention of the Common Market countries." W. Wirski, *Zycie Gospodarcze,* August 11–18, 1963. For extended discussion, see V. Pavlat, "EEC and East-West Trade," *Mirovaia Ekonomika i Mezhdunarodnie Otnosheniia,* No. 11, 1963.

came a matter of widespread discussion, and actual trade again reached the levels of 1948) the total trade with OECD countries approximately doubled and in the case of some communist states has come to assume an important place in their economies (see Table III). Incomplete data for 1964 indicate a further average annual increase of about 10% in the total value of trade with the West. Thus by 1964 Rumania's trade with the West accounted for about 35% of its total trade or just a little less than the Polish percentage. On the communist side almost one-half of the total value of trade with the West was carried by the USSR, followed by Poland with about 15% and with Rumania moving up fast; on the Western side, no one state predominated, although West Germany led with about 30% of the total NATO trade with the communist countries, followed by the United Kingdom (about 18%), Italy (12%), and France (under 11%).

The increase in East-West trade was encouraged by a gradual liberalization in quota restrictions previously imposed by the West and by a shift from annual to three-year trade agreements in most cases. Both steps went far in meeting long-standing communist grievances. For example, until 1964 most imports to the United Kingdom from East Europe were subject to quotas defined annually. Only raw materials were excepted from these restrictions and could be imported freely under a general license arrangement. But in 1964 negotiations were conducted in order to liberalize quota restrictions applicable to British trade with Bulgaria, Czechoslovakia, Hungary, Poland, and Rumania in order to reduce the number of commodities subject to the quota, leaving it applicable to those items the import of which would be likely to cause serious dislocations in the British economy. Since 1959 the bulk of the British trade with the Soviet Union has been under an open general license arrangement, with only about 10% of imports subject to quota negotiations. Similar agreements to expand and facilitate trade have been signed by West Germany with several East European states. They provided for direct increases in volume and their three-year life span assured that such trade will henceforth be less subject to annual fluctuations.[11] Agreements of this kind were concluded also by Benelux, France, and Italy providing for considerable increases in their trade with East Europe.* The American-Rumanian agreement of June 1964, while not impressive in terms of volume, was also of importance in that it set the precedent for purchases in the United States of industrial equipment and installations with U.S.-facilitated credit guarantees.

In the early sixties, however, East-West trade, while growing, was still relatively small. The trade of most Western countries with the Soviet Union and East Europe involved only a small portion of their total trade (see Table IV), the exceptions being Greece and Iceland (with the Soviet Union and Eastern Europe accounting for approximately 20% of the exports and 8% of the imports of Greece, and 19% of the exports and 18% of the imports of Iceland.) Symptomatic of the disrupture of Europe's prewar trade patterns was the fact that Franco-Russian trade did not reach its 1913 level again until 1958,[12] while Polish trade with the West European countries of the Common Market, which in 1938 accounted for 39% of total Polish trade, made up only 9% of the total Polish trade in 1963.† At that time the value of EEC exports to CEMA countries was 10% less than in 1938 and imports 20% less,[13] a reduction which is all the more striking considering the general expansion of volume and value of international trade. Communist countries still traded predominantly with one another (see Table V).

While the fundamental cause of this state of affairs is to be found in the original Soviet decision to impose on East Europe the rejection of the Marshall Plan, it is perpetuated now by other political and economic factors. For primarily political reasons the communist states for a long time simply

---

* For example, Italian-Rumanian trade in 1964 is to exceed by 20% the 1963 level.
† "Poland's Trade Exchange with the Countries of the Common Market," *Rynki Zagraniczne*, May 23, 1964. The corresponding percentages for trade with Germany were in 1938 23% of Polish imports and 24.1% of exports, while in 1963 3% of imports and 5% of exports.

ignored the emergence of such institutions as GATT (General Agreement on Tariffs and Trade) and the Common Market. Eight years after the formation of EEC, they have been unwilling to accredit ambassadors to it although the lack of direct communication obviously affects negatively their own economic interests and hinders the further development of trade between East and West.*

The Soviet approach to the problem of international trade has been marked by considerable duplicity, proceeding from the subordination of economic to political considerations. The Soviet Union has been more interested in disrupting the relations between EEC and EFTA than in striving to normalize trade relations between the East and the West. As late as February 1964, for essentially propagandistic reasons designed to appeal to the less developed countries, the Soviet Union was proposing that GATT be replaced by another world organization, and it exacted the support of both Poland and Czechoslovakia for this proposal, notwithstanding their interest in collaborating with GATT. Not surprisingly, communist participation in GATT, not to speak of the International Monetary Fund (of which only Yugoslavia is a member and from which such states as Algeria or Ghana have benefited), has been very limited. The political objective of disrupting or preventing Western multilateralism has prevailed over the collective or even the individual economic needs of the communist states.†

* Trade agreements between European members of EEC and the communist states have a provision for annual renegotiation in the event that obligations to the Common Market, particularly in the terms of its common commercial policy, render changes in the treaties necessary. This is done by a formal statement on the part of the West European signatory power, which is annexed to the treaty. Although the East does not formally recognize this statement, it has acquiesced in its being made; therefore the statement is a form of indirect recognition. The 1963 EEC offers to the Russians to cut tariffs on four items which are important Russian exports to the West was in part designed to force the Russians to recognize the Community by making a direct response to it, but by early 1965 the Russians had still refrained from making a direct response.

† The Soviet economic pressure on Finland in late 1958 and early 1959 and on Austria provides incidentally an illustration of the Soviet willingness to use close economic ties for political motives.

Political considerations apart, there have also been major economic obstacles to East-West trade. The East simply did not have enough products suitable for export to the West to meet its import requirements. The new East European industry could not compete on the Western markets while the agricultural exports were encountering the new Common Market tariffs. The Soviet Union has had some success with its oil sales, and it could also take advantage of its gold for purchases in the West. Its potentially enormous market offered attractive opportunities, especially for those Western firms specializing in the delivery of complete plant facilities (e.g., Krupp). Nonetheless, the Soviet Union also required credit for any appreciable expansion in its trade with the developed Western countries, given its relatively limited opportunities for export of industrial goods to the West. Soviet spokesmen made no secret of the fact that substantial credits were therefore essential.

East-West trade is thus still much more important to the East than to the West. The exceptions are Britain and Italy: the industrial overexpansion in northern Italy as well as the need to pay for Italian oil imports, and the competitive pressures from the new Japanese and German industries felt by some British concerns has given Italy and Britain some genuine economic interest in the expansion of trade with the East.* Otherwise, East-West trade has not been a major Western economic preoccupation, and it plays a relatively minor role in its total trade.† For the East, trade with the West has been a unique source of industrial imports; for the West it has been mainly a source of nonindustrial items, many of which (such as oil or tobacco) are available from other places. That this problem has afflicted both the Soviet Union

---

* The Italian-Soviet trade agreement of February 1964, valid for five years, provides for an annual increase in trade of about 10%.

† Compare the percentages of trade to the total trade of the two sides in Tables III and IV, and for country to country ratios, see my "The Soviet Union, the Common Market, and France," in Sydney Fisher, ed., *The European Community and France,* Ohio State University Press, 1965. In 1963 3.6% of EEC imports and 3.2% of the exports involved trade with the Soviet Union and East Europe; for EFTA, 4.2% and 4.5% respectively.

and the East European countries, is shown by Table VI. A country-by-country analysis of chief items of trade in 1962 indicates that in most cases, the principal items of Western imports have been nonindustrial; the principal Western exports to individual communist states have been industrial. Moreover, these exports have been those of critical importance to more sophisticated industry: machine tools, precision instruments, electrical machinery, and synthetics.[14]

Thus, from the point of view of the East, the ideal would be an expansion of trade with the West, necessarily through Western credits, thereby increasing the flow of Western industrial products to the communist countries. These would be paid for in part by the export to the West of raw materials from the East, acquired in part also by the communist states from the developing countries in exchange for machinery from the communist countries. From the communist standpoint, such a triangular arrangement would overcome the competitive difficulties which face the communist industrial products in the Western markets, and would also have the *political and ideological* advantage of making the communist states the chief promoters of the industrial development of the new nations, in part through indirect Western aid. It is noteworthy that Soviet exports of machinery and industrial equipment to developing countries rose from 4.8% of the total Soviet exports to these countries in 1955 to 50.4% in 1962, and in value from $5.4 million to $285.9 million.[15] This was generally true of the East European communist states, and paralleled the simultaneous increase in communist imports of Western industrial products.

Another important impediment to East-West trade involves the very nature of the communist economic system and the difficulty it poses for closer relations, particularly with the Common Market. Until such time as the communist states are prepared to revise their system of state monopoly in foreign trade, which involves a complex network of long-term bilateral trade arrangements and commodity exchanges, complicated clearing schemes, absence of price criteria for determining currency exchanges and which is, as a result, both rigid and incapable of flexible response to market changes, it is doubtful that a very significant development in East-West trade can take place. Western Europe, only now in the process of painfully working out the complexities of freer trade among its own members, is not likely to take a backward step by developing extensive links with states which rigidly control their foreign trade. A proper climate for Western businessmen in the communist states has first to be created: easy access to economic leaders and to economic data, opportunities to inspect factories. These are normal features of international trade which in communist countries have been inhibited by a tradition of secrecy and suspicion.[16]

There are indications, however, that the desire of the communist East European states to increase their trade with the West has already compelled some of them to revise gradually their earlier negative attitude toward such international bodies as GATT, an organization designed to lower trade barriers, to set common standards for international trade and to eliminate discriminatory trade practices. Although GATT rules are not well adapted for state trading, the organization does provide a useful forum under the guidance of certain broad principles for the discussion of trade problems. Of the communist states only Czechoslovakia was formally a member, having joined prior to the 1948 coup, but its actual participation was nil. Yugoslavia joined in 1962 (initially becoming a provisional member), having earlier arranged for its foreign trade to be handled by several trade companies, operating with import licenses and free to make their own foreign purchases. In effect, this involved a limited adoption of the market economy. Poland submitted its candidature in 1959. Even though Poland failed to meet GATT requirements, it was permitted to participate in the preparations for the "Kennedy round," admitted to the agriculture committee, and finally allowed to participate in the "Kennedy round" deliberations. In the summer of 1964 Rumania also began to explore the possibility of association and eventually membership. The Polish and Rumanian efforts, pointing to increased communist participation in GATT, were a modest but desirable step forward toward the elimination of essentially political and ideological obstructions to world trade.*

These changes in attitude suggest that economic pressures were capable of profoundly changing earlier communist views and practices. Indeed, these external changes have been paralleled by domestic reforms. The climate surrounding Western businessmen in East Europe and Russia improved enormously during the early sixties. Some of the East European states, notably Poland and Czechoslovakia, began to revise their foreign trade structure, and it is to be expected that all the communist states will do likewise. But precisely because these changes were finally occurring only under the pressure of economic necessity, nothing would be more likely to dissipate this desirable trend than a Western competition in granting credits to the communist states. Yet such competition has been in the making. The British have flatly stated the view that credit is a strictly commercial matter to be decided on a nondiscriminatory basis according to the type of goods to be covered and the credit rating of the importer. In the spring of 1964 Czechoslovakia obtained a 12-year British credit for the purchase of fertilizer plants and in July the Soviet Union was granted a 15-year credit for the purchase of chemicals. These British accommodations, guaranteed by the government, immediately set off pressure from French financial circles favoring a positive response to the Soviet request for 15-year credits for the purchase of heavy industrial and additional chemical plant equipment.[17] French sources also reported that

---

* That these steps encountered many internal obstacles is suggested by the curt Bulgarian denial of a story that Bulgaria was also seeking access to GATT. (Sofia BTA, official statement, July 3, 1964.) For a discussion of the role of GATT with respect to East-West trade, see William Diebold in *East-West Trade*, Committee on Foreign Relations, United States Senate, November 1964, pp. 233–236.

American firms were being encouraged by government authorities to develop closer contacts with the East European states and that after the November 1964 elections the way would be open for using the facilities of the Export-Import Bank for financing purposes.[18] The American and EEC positions have been to restrict credits to five years, but although the United States has been attempting to persuade its allies not to exceed this limit, pressure from interested firms is likely to increase. As a result, the communist states will find it increasingly easy to obtain Western credits for the purchase of needed industrial items.

The communist elites would like to lift the Iron Curtain in economics while leaving it down in cultural-social affairs. They demand closer economic contacts with the West, and even credits, while still preaching the economic superiority of their own systems, maintaining political restrictions on the development of contacts between European peoples, promising the developing countries that with communist aid they will surpass the West, and aiding Cuba or North Vietnam in their revolutionary ventures. In this context, it would perhaps be appropriate for the West to reiterate its own stand that its attitude toward economic relations must depend in part on the extent to which the communist states are willing to make adjustments in their cultural-social Iron Curtain policies and in their own foreign trade practices.

According to Common Market experts, agricultural policy toward the East is the area in which some opportunities for mutual adjustment exist once the common agricultural policies of the West have taken shape. Beyond that, little thought has been given in the Common Market to the future pattern of East-West relationships. Although the Common Market desires recognition from the East, there is some internal division on the question of whether the East should be entitled to some concessions in return for extending diplomatic recognition to the community. The predominant position is that it is not so entitled and that it should be made to feel that recognition is in the East European and Soviet interest. The 1963 offer of reduced tariffs to Russia was made not only to elicit a direct Russian response and therefore recognition but also as a point of departure for reciprocal concessions from the Russians. Otherwise, there is a singular lack of long-range political planning in the Common Market with respect to the East European problem. As a result, the political implications of the development of the Common Market tend to be neglected.

It is unlikely that at the present time a tightly coordinated Western policy is possible (especially since it was difficult to arrange even at the time of the Stalinist threat), although eventually the Common Market may move in that direction. Apart from the economic complications caused by the British rupture of the five-year limit on credits to the East, the formation of a common commercial policy is presently also complicated by De Gaulle who, primarily for political reasons, moved away from the five-year limit by granting seven-year credits to the Soviet Union in October 1964. Present indications point to America and Germany holding the line on the five-year credits toward the Soviet Union, but with probable modifications in the case of the East European states. The Soviets realize this and have been using their breakthrough in Britain and elsewhere in the hope of stimulating competitive pressures in Germany and America (neither of which is presently under major economic stress to expand that trade), since a major expansion in East-West trade largely depends on their willingness to extend large-scale credits.

The Ideological Neutrality of Industrial Development

The communists have justified the division of Europe— and the Iron Curtain—in part by the argument that it was essential for the industrialization of East Europe and its liberation from economic dependence on the West. At the same time they also claim that the communist model of industrialization is historically superior—i.e., more rapid. These two claims have become an essential part of the communist rationalization of their monopoly of power in East Europe and have gained widespread currency abroad, endowing the communist system with a certain amount of prestige, especially in the developing nations.

The East European industrialization itself has yielded impressive fruits. It is to be remembered that it involved not only communist ambitions but also a genuinely patriotic commitment on the part of many East Europeans anxious to modernize their hitherto backward countries (devastated by World War II). East Europe viewed as a whole has, to use a phrase that has gained widespread acceptance, "taken off" in sustained economic growth. Nonetheless, the record does not justify the frequent communist claims for the superiority of their economic system. In fact, a cursory comparison of the development of several Western and Eastern European countries which in 1938 were at very generally approximate levels of economic development and/or which were at a comparable level in specific productions (for example, steel, which the communists have stressed) testifies to the "neutrality" of economic development and justifies neither side's claims of ideological superiority in industrialization. Tables VII-XV, while encompassing only a few comparable areas of production of the various countries and excluding items in which one or the other side has a traditional specialization (e.g., Greek shipping or automobiles in the West) or a special resource advantage (Polish coal), reveal a basic uniformity in the pace of development and industrialization.*

* It is to be noted that communist spokesmen have often compared Poland and Italy and that in the early fifties they claimed that Poland would surpass Italy in economic development by the beginning of this decade; Austria and Hungary are relatively similar in size, population, resources, and level of development; *mutatis mutandis,* so are Spain, Rumania, and Yugoslavia, although Spain's population is larger; while Czechoslovakia and Sweden represent examples of higher level of development. (A comparison of Czechoslovakia and Benelux might have been an alternative, since Czechoslovakia is closer in population to it than to Sweden, but the Benelux is a much more industrially advanced region and the comparison

These tables suggest that the communist pattern of development and modernization in Europe is not remarkably more successful than has been the case elsewhere in Europe, without the communist systems' coercive mobilization, but neither is it strikingly inferior. The communist-imposed model of the "command economy"-type of development involved enormous sacrifices on the part of the East Europeans. Industrialization was conducted in the context of intense political terror, forced savings extracted from the people, especially from the peasants, extensive Soviet exploitation of formerly allied countries, such as Czechoslovakia and Poland, and the extraction of large-scale reparations from such former enemies as Rumania, Hungary, Bulgaria, and East Germany.

To be sure, this coercive mobilization made up for the lack of capital which was infused into the Western countries by the Marshall Plan, but participation in the Plan had been opened to the communist states and they chose not to enter into it. (Incidentally, it should be noted that Spain also did not benefit from the Marshall Plan.) Considering the repeated communist assertions that the Soviet Union was aiding the development of East Europe and that the communist pattern of economic development allegedly was historically "superior," the absence of a clear-cut superiority in the industrial sphere (not to mention comparative communist failures in agricultural growth * and in personal consumption [19]) was bound to undermine the ideological underpinnings of the communist position in East Europe.

---

would have been unfair to Czechoslovakia.) Comparisons could also be made between Greece and Bulgaria and the Benelux and East Germany.

To allay the suspicion that data were selected to make a point, it should be noted that the respective countries first were matched and the items for comparison were selected; only then were the data compiled. Obviously, by selecting the data first it would have been possible to demonstrate the "superiority" of either side.

* Since the war, agricultural production in West Europe has risen by approximately 25%; in East Europe, by 5%. L. A. Dellin, "Agriculture and the Peasant in East Europe," in F. Galati, ed., *East Europe in the Sixties*, New York, 1963, pp. 66–67.

Furthermore, since there is no longer the danger that certain Western monopolies will again acquire the dominant and even exploitative position that some did enjoy in East Europe of the pre-World War II period, the argument that East Europe needs to be cordoned off from West Europe for its own protection no longer generates a positive response among the nationalistically inclined East Europeans.

The preceding argument is reinforced by a comprehensive study in comparative economic development, published in 1963 in Poland.[20] Although controversial in some respects,[21] it provides a much wider framework for justifying similar conclusions. Taking steel as the basic index for measuring industrial growth, its author presents detailed comparative data showing that Soviet industrialization was in fact only marginally more rapid than the pace achieved in Russia just prior to World War I;[22] that the per capita progress in the production of steel in Russia and Japan in 1928–1940, with both starting at almost the same per capita level and engaging in strenuous efforts to increase their production, was strikingly similar;* that the pace of Soviet postwar recovery in steel production again paralleled the levels attained in noncommunist countries;[23] that there is a uniformity in the postwar increase in the steel production obtained by the Soviet bloc and by West Europe; † and that the rate of acceleration in the per capita production of steel over the last century and a half involves increasingly compressed but regular phases, applicable after 1917 to both communist and noncommunist societies.[24] These findings led the author to conclude, much to the indignation of his communist reviewers, that economic growth is determined primarily by technological acceleration and therefore by nonideological considerations.

European experience with industrialization also refutes

---

* For example, the per capita steel production in the USSR in 1929 was 32 kg.; in Japan in 1928 it was 30 kg. Eleven years later, it was 96 and 90 respectively. Kurowski, *op. cit.*, pp. 134–38.

† Taking 1946 as 100, the figures for 1960 were 510 and 470 respectively; 1950 as 100, they were 240 and 242 respectively. *Ibid.*, p. 178.

the established "Leninist law" of the uneven development of capitalist societies, according to which contradictions between the privileged and the unprivileged intensify under capitalism. The spectacular industrial development of Italy in the West, more rapid than that of the more developed states, and of Rumania in the East, significantly more rapid than that of either East Germany or Czechoslovakia, suggests that the contrary is true on both sides [25]—and incidentally it puts in a rather awkward position those East German and Czech economists who, basing themselves on the argument of "efficiency," argued against the industrial development of Rumania, in effect propounding for the communist camp nothing less than the equivalent of the "law of uneven development."

The nonideological character of industrial development thus threatens the ideological structure that reinforces the present political division of Europe. In the context of the return of international politics to East Europe, the preoccupation of the East European elites with the further economic growth of their own countries is already undermining the communist bloc orientation, with its traditionally Leninist dichotomic image of the world. Speaking in 1964 at the United Nations World Trade Conference in Geneva, the Rumanian delegate proposed that members be grouped "with regard to their level of development regardless of their respective social or trade system." In effect, he was suggesting the primacy of the economic factor over the ideological, since the implementation of his proposal would have been to put the highly industrialized Czechoslovakia and the Soviet Union (and perhaps West Germany) in one camp, and Rumania or Bulgaria (and perhaps Portugal) in another.

It would be dangerous to underestimate the degree to which certain basic ideological prejudices have become imbedded in the social fabric, existing institutions, personal perspectives, not to speak of vested interests.* However, the trend

---

* For other factors prompting erosion, such as nuclear weapons, as well as for an extended discussion of the sources of ideological vitality, see my *Ideology and*

seems to favor strongly a more domestically oriented ideological perspective—in brief, domesticism and not universalism, relativism and not absolutism. This increased emphasis on domestic considerations is likely to make the communist elites seek ways out of their economic dilemmas without too much regard for the ideologically influenced dichotomic image of the world and doctrinaire economic practices. They may place a higher value on improving rapidly the standard of living of their peoples, unnecessarily depressed by the communist pattern of industrialization that was deliberately undertaken without any cooperation with the West. Symptomatic is the realization already spreading among communist economists that the command-type of economy has become inappropriate to the higher stage of industrialization now achieved and that further decentralization and eventually even some market-type devices will have to be introduced.[26]

In Europe, politics and economics both conspire against the communist ideology and portend the erosion of its universalist perspectives. European politics reflect the renewed vitality of nation-states; European economics underline the ideological neutrality of the technological revolution. They present opportunities for the lifting of the social and cultural Iron Curtain by the use of enlightened trade policies. The gradual subordination of ideological to domestic considerations may still leave paramount the political and power factors that caused the partition of Europe. But the erosion may gradually open the way to dealing with these political factors on their own terms, unaffected by the emotional and absolutizing consequences of ideological dogmas.

Power in Soviet Politics, New York, 1962. Also for a comparison of the staying power of ideological views in America and Russia, see Z. Brzezinski and S. Huntington, *Political Power: USA/USSR,* New York, 1964, esp. Chapter I.

CHAPTER THREE

The European Stalemate

Postwar Europe has seen the failure of the offensive policies of the East and the West. The Soviet Union did not expand politically or militarily to the Atlantic. The United States did not "liberate" a single communist state and passively observed the crushing of two initially successful anti-Soviet rebellions. Increasingly, the postures of the two sides in Europe have come to resemble two bulls that have locked their horns in battle: neither mortally wounded, both tired of the fight, both unable to disengage, neither able to take the first step without fear of providing a tempting target for a blow from the other. Although no one was willing to accept the European stalemate, all had to live with it. Some wanted to change it drastically, others only a little, and some, others suspected, were really willing to accept it but did not say so. The interplay between the changing European reality and the contradictory policies within alliances and between them made the European stalemate inherently unstable.

Soviet Policy: Frustration on the Central Front

To the Soviets, Europe is still the "central front" in the confrontation with the West. This basic assumption has guided Soviet policy since World War II. It has been systematized and amplified in the course of the Sino-Soviet debate during which the Chinese advanced the counterproposition that the underdeveloped world, especially the "national liberation" struggle, has become the arena for the historically decisive showdown with "U.S. imperialism." * The Soviet position stressed instead the primacy of the direct competition between the developed parts of the two global systems. In the Soviet view the eventual economic supremacy of the communist world, and hence its increased military power, will jointly—albeit peacefully—effect a qualitative turn in world history. Thus, while the battles in the Third World are important, they are peripheral to the direct confrontation on the central front. Europe, the western parts supported by the United States, the eastern part linked to the Soviet Union, is where history will be shaped.†

In the years 1958–62 the Soviet Union pursued in Europe a *policy of breakthrough,* exemplified dramatically by renewed pressure on Berlin. At first after Stalin's death the Soviet leaders, absorbed by their domestic struggles, had sought a partial detente in Europe, the so-called "spirit of Geneva," and had agreed to the Austrian peace treaty. By 1958, however, the worst phases of the de-Stalinization campaign were over, the Chinese pressure for more vigorous action was rising, American policy, with Dulles fading, seemed adrift, and, above all, Soviet military power was enhanced by the launching of the first Soviet ICBM's. It was in that context that the Soviet leaders launched the new campaign to coerce the West out of Berlin, through sustained military-political pressure.

The long-range effect of this policy, if successful, would

* "The national liberation revolution in Asia, Africa, and Latin America now emerges as the most important force which inflicts a direct blow on imperialism. Asia, Africa, and Latin America are the regions in which the contradictions of the world are concentrated." *Jen-Minh Jih-Pao,* October 22, 1963.

† See *Pravda,* January 7, 1963; M. Suslov, *Report to the Central Committee,* CPSU, February 14, 1964; and *Pravda,* April 28, 1964. For a good procommunist commentary, see L. Gorz, "The Sino-Soviet Debate," *Les Temps Modernes,* May 1963. In the suggestive words of a sympathetic critic, the Chinese theory reflects "a respect for subjective factors, for men; there is there a mentality of a militant, of an organizer of the masses." By way of contrast, the Soviet approach is said to reveal "an immense respect for objective factors, for things; there is there a mentality of a technician, of an organizer of production." Claude Cadart, "On the Crisis of the International Communist Movement," *Les Temps Modernes,* p. 1981.

have been a political breakthrough to the West. It would have refuted the viability of NATO and might have produced first in Germany and then elsewhere a demoralizing atmosphere of defeatism. The stakes were so high that in the pursuit of their goal Soviet leaders adopted Dulles' earlier policy of brinkmanship, with the result that by 1960 and 1961 fears of an imminent nuclear showdown had become widespread.* Sustained pressure was applied until the Cuban confrontation of October 1962. It appears that the Soviet leaders, faced in Europe with a firm yet passive American response, were unwilling to test directly the limits of American self-restraint and by the emplacement of missiles in Cuba attempted to stage the setting for an indirect showdown and eventual quid pro quo.[1] The unexpected U.S. reaction in Cuba led the Soviet Union to a general reevaluation of the East-West relationship and to the conclusion that a direct breakthrough in Europe could not be effected.

Unwilling to accept the Chinese analysis, the Soviet leaders, after approximately a year of fumbling and drift, apparently concluded that their immediate interests would be better served by an amelioration in American-Soviet relations, resulting perhaps in an American acceptance of the status quo in Europe. The unstable condition of Soviet power in Eastern Europe gave this policy a particular urgency; an American-Soviet co-sponsorship of the division on the Elbe underlining the acceptance by the West of Soviet hegemony over East Europe would have been a most welcome reinforcement for the Soviet position. Improved relations could also establish a climate for more extensive economic ties—a matter of some importance in view of the Soviet and East European

* At this time the Soviet leaders were showering the Europeans with crude threats; typical was Khrushchev's own account to the Moscow workers: "I told the Greek Ambassador that the most sensible policy for Greece was to withdraw from NATO. Then, if war broke out, Greece would not suffer. The Ambassador told me: 'I trust the Chairman of the Council of Ministers of the Soviet Union never to give the order to drop atomic bombs on the Akropolis and other historical monuments of Greece.' Mr. Ambassador, I would not want to disappoint you, but you are deeply mistaken." *Pravda*, August 12, 1961.

economic difficulties. Most important of all, the new American-Soviet relationship would serve as a point of departure for a new *policy of fragmentation,* which by 1963–64 had emerged as a substitute for the earlier head-on attempt to change by threats of force the existing political configuration in Europe.

The policy of fragmentation had basically two objectives: to weaken—but probably not to destroy—the American-European relationship and to undermine West European political and economic unity. Although the Soviets have been constant in their desire to undermine European unity, their attitude toward the American position in Europe had become more ambivalent out of fear that the alternative might be a more militant Franco-German concert. Accordingly, the Soviet leaders strove to abet inter-European divisions. Conflict in the West not only delays the emergence of the Common Market as a unifying force, but it also revitalizes the Marxist-Leninist belief that capitalism contains inherent contradictions. Furthermore, a divided Europe is likely to remain dominated by the United States, and this permits direct Soviet-American negotiations about its future. The Soviet leaders saw the United States as basically sharing the USSR's interest in preserving the European status quo.* Therefore, if European unity could not be thwarted, the Soviets wanted to ensure that Europeans unity was at least offset by European-American conflicts. The USSR wanted to avoid any possibility that a united Europe would first reject the status quo and then persuade the United States to support European ambitions. If an American-European conflict eventually were to reduce the American willingness to defend vital European interests, that would be better yet.†

* This led the Chinese, propagating their "second intermediate zone" (see supra p. 45), to charge the Soviets with abandoning the struggle to drive the United States out of Europe and even with helping the United States to consolidate its position. "Two Different Lines on the Question of War and Peace," *Jen-Minh Jih-Pao,* November 19, 1963.

† In a perceptive article, a Soviet author suggested late in 1963 that: 1) The Bonn-Paris axis was the most anti-Soviet formation; 2) the USA will try to

Soviet foreign policy commentators have openly discussed the general outlines of the policy of fragmentation. In
Soviet eyes De Gaulle, in spite of the anti-Soviet edge of his
attempt to forge a German-French coalition, appeared as a
useful instrument for paralyzing the European drive for unity.
As such, in the short run, he was to be encouraged. At the
same time they professed to see a welcome shift to the left
among European socialists, strengthening the hopes for West
European neutralism.[2] This led them to the formulation of a
two-pincers strategy: "It is quite possible that the cold war bul-
warks will not be first eroded in the center but on the fringes
of Europe—Scandinavia, the South-East, the Balkans."[3]

In keeping with this analysis the years 1963–64 saw
vigorous Soviet diplomatic activity: a trip to Scandinavia in
June 1964 by the Soviet Prime Minister, punctuated by blunt
advocacy of neutralism for the area; proposals for the dimili-
tarization of the Mediterranean;[*] visits to France by Party
secretary and politburo member Podgorny and by the then
Izvestia editor Adzubei and a visit to Italy by Mr. Kosygin,
presidium member and the then deputy prime minister. Their
objective: France and the United States were to be encouraged
to checkmate each other: Germany was to be isolated; and
West Europe was to be outflanked by neutralism in the north
and in the south.

The East European states could play a very useful role
in promoting this new policy of fragmentation. Poland, for
example, could be helpful in influencing Scandinavian or English public opinion. Hungary could play on old ties with

combat it by shifting from the United Kingdom as its chief ally to West Germany,
a course said to be advocated by Acheson; 3) Bonn was using the Paris-Bonn
axis to get nuclear weapons; 4) De Gaulle was not really interested in German
reunification but saw in the Paris-Bonn axis a way of influencing U.S. policy.
I. Lemin, "A Foreign Policy of the United States: The Crisis of Post-War Policy
and the Struggle of Contradictory Tendencies," *Mirovaia Ekonomika i Mezhdunarodnie Otnosheniia*, No. 10, 1963.
* Otherwise "the Mediterranean could become a dead sea in every sense of the
word," stated the Soviet note, impartially expressing concern for the safety of
religious centers in the Vatican, Jerusalem, Mecca, and Medina (May 20, 1963).

Austria. The East European states in general could be more effective than the Soviet Union in overcoming Western barriers to trade in view of Western sympathy for the East Europeans. But from the Soviet point of view, it was important that these approaches should not create a feed-back effect, stimulating an Eastern European thirst for more independent policies. Firm control of East Germany, sealing off Poland and partially Czechoslovakia, could provide some reassurance on that score.

In view of the abandonment of the policy of breakthrough, the threat to sign a "peace treaty" with East Germany was quietly dropped. However, for the Soviets, East Germany remained a vital outpost in the very center of Europe, geographically, militarily, and politically sealing off direct access to East Europe from the West. The Soviet stake in East Germany, furthermore, has grown with the industrial development of the area, and by 1962 East Germany, in spite of its small population and size, had become the Soviet Union's most important trading partner, accounting for more than one-sixth of the Soviet Union's total world trade and for almost three times as much as the Soviet trade with all EEC countries.[4] More important still, East Germany was the chief Soviet supplier of vitally needed complex industrial machinery, while the Soviet drive to develop its chemical industry, on which much of the present Soviet economic development relies, was heavily dependent on deliveries from the East German chemical industries.[*] Economic as well as political considerations thus underlined the Soviet stake in East Germany. To emphasize the point the Soviet Union signed in June 1964 a treaty of friendship with the Ulbricht regime, a step taken with respect to the other East European nations more than a decade earlier. The much threatened "peace treaty" had been designed to unsettle the status quo in Central Europe; the suddenly pro-

[*] Only 3.5% of the Soviet exports to East Germany were of industrial character—which underlines the industrial importance of East Germany. See *Razvitie Narodnovo Khoziaistva Germanskoi Demokraticheskoi Respubliki*, Moscow, 1959, pp. 643–644.

claimed "friendship treaty" was meant to solidify the outer edge of Soviet-dominated Europe.

The policy of fragmentation is still basically an offensive policy. It is calculated not to ease the division of Europe, but to divide the noncommunist half. It reflects a deep-seated Soviet inability to come to terms with the notion that Europe can unite and that the East will have to develop a stable relationship with this emerging new Europe. The Soviet reactions to the appearance of the Common Market are a case in point. They show how ideological blinders have distorted the Soviet perception of European developments and how they prompted the Soviet Union to adopt policies that perhaps were not even in its own best interests. In this respect, the East European communist elites, presumably because of their peoples' traditionally closer ties with the West, are somewhat ahead of the Soviet Union in appreciating the real nature of western European developments.

The Soviet Union had justified its opposition to the Marshall Plan, which the East Europeans had wanted to join, on the grounds that the Plan was meant to restore Germany as an economic power and to subjugate Eastern Europe. It further predicted that one consequence of the Plan would be the permanent political subordination of Europe to America. The Soviet Union persisted in this attitude even with respect to the formation of the Common Market. Thus, broadly speaking, immediately prior to the Treaty of Rome of March 1957 and for a while afterwards, Soviet spokesmen and analysts stressed the proposition that the Common Market politically was an American plot to subordinate Europe, while economically it was unimportant. The Treaty was seen by Soviet observers as expressing an inherent tendency toward domination "by one leading imperialist power over others," [5] and leading toward "American tutelage over France and the whole of Western Europe." [6] As a result, the West European countries would be "robbed" of any possibility of pursuing an independent economic policy.[7] Quite remarkably for analysts steeped in the Marxist doctrine, very little attention was paid to the economic aspects of the undertaking. Attention was focused on the more ideologically satisfactory matter of the "sharpening of contradictions" in Western Europe. The prevailing view was that these contradictions were fundamentally insoluble and that the Common Market would founder on them.[8]

In the late fifties, the emphasis shifted politically to the German threat (a variant of this shift was the argument stressing a joint American-German hegemony), while economically the Common Market was seen in an ambivalent light. It was no longer simply dismissed as an insignificant irrelevance, but it was not yet taken seriously. The Common Market was represented as a joint American-German conspiracy, designed particularly to denigrate France. Numerous articles appeared in Soviet journals "proving" that West German monopolies were extending their sway over all of West Europe, and providing the underpinning for American political supremacy. The irreconcilability of French and German national interests was a constant leitmotiv. Even after General de Gaulle had come to power, the above view continued to dominate.

In the early sixties, a sense of uncertainty and ambivalence pervaded Soviet political analyses, especially when defining the Soviet stand toward English participation in the Common Market. In economics, the earlier ambivalence gave way to at best thinly veiled fears of the Common Market's impact on the communist world. By the middle of 1962 the Soviet leaders seem to have awakened to the realization that the Common Market was a reality. Overcompensating perhaps for their past belief in its "insoluble internal contradictions," they now began to speak of it as a powerful and dangerous instrument of imperialist aggression.[9]

The Soviet leadership was thus in a predicament: from the economic point of view, England's membership in the Common Market would be a further denial of the underlying premises of their ideological perspective because it would round out an even more powerful capitalist economic world; in addition it would be certain to have a further negative impact on Soviet and communist East European trade. Perhaps even more important, it would intensify the historical appeal of European unity, fortifying the revisionist mood among the youth of East Europe and even Russia. At the same time, from a political point of view something would be gained if Britain joined. Germany would be balanced; a restraining voice, perhaps eventually even a pacifist one, would be introduced (so the Soviets might have reasoned) into the political councils of the Common Market; the entire political structure would become more complex.[10] As Moscow belatedly began to perceive that a Franco-German axis was being formed,[11] Britain looked like a good counterweight.[12]

From the second half of 1962 Soviet political analysts began to lay primary emphasis on the Franco-German threat, while in the economic domain they were welcoming the open manifestations of "imperialist contradictions." Soviet dogmas were given a new lease on life by General de Gaulle's press conference of January 14, 1963, excluding the United Kingdom from the Common Market. Triumphantly proclaiming that "this confirms what Marxists have said all along: underneath the thin crust of 'Atlantic unity' there boils the hot lava of imperialist contradictions,"[13] the Soviets for the time being laid aside their fears of Franco-German imperialism and saw in this renewed proof of the West's inevitable decline. The whole Western alliance was represented as being at stake. Though Soviet reporting on the whole took a sympathetic tone toward Britain's plight, the dominant note was clearly one of jubilation.

But soon more somber voices were also heard. V. Nekrasov, writing in *Izvestia,* warned his readers that Britain's exclusion facilitated the transformation of the Common Market into a political-military bloc, and by the end of 1963 the traditional assertions concerning "irreconcilable contradictions" in the West had become more muted.[14] Indeed, by the spring of 1964 Soviet diplomats were reported to be making discreet inquiries concerning the advantages of diplomatic relations with EEC.[15] These were accompanied by renewed efforts to established contact with De Gaulle, especially after the cooling in French-German relations. Moscow presumably hoped to take advantage of De Gaulle's assertiveness to impede European integration, even though it conceded that the long-range danger to the Soviet security stemmed precisely from De Gaulle's vision of a Europe led by France and Germany.

The Soviet reactions illustrated Moscow's persisting inclination to gamble on short-range tactical gains, even at the cost of more basic but distant interests.* More important still, the inadequacy of the Soviet appraisal of the Common Market revealed the continuing influence of ideological perspectives, particularly with regard to the hallowed doctrine of "inherent capitalist contradictions." [16] These ideological biases were reinforced by the deeply felt national fear that a united West Europe would become an instrument of German ambitions, to be used against Russia. It is difficult to assess the degree to which Soviet policy-makers were actually influenced by the fear of Germany, but that fear, fed by West German rearmament and by communist propaganda, was certainly widespread among the Russian and East European peoples, and hence permeated also the ruling communist elites.

The perpetuation of the division of Germany is thus the linchpin of the Soviet efforts to promote both Soviet security

* For some parallels to the equally shortsighted Soviet reactions to EDC and the MLF, see my "Moscow and the MLF: Hostility and Ambivalence," *Foreign Affairs*, October 1964. Soviet policy toward German rearmament bears a striking resemblance to a self-fulfilling prophecy. The direct consequence of the first Berlin crisis and the Korean war was to strengthen the American view, already widespread among the military, that West Germany must be rearmed; the subsequent defeat of EDC (with the French Communist Party playing a major role in it) made the reappearance of a national German army a certainty. The second Berlin crisis, in its turn, intensified the European, including West German, demands for some participation in the disposal of nuclear weapons, thereby bringing West Germany closer to membership in the nuclear club. Yet the Soviet opposition to the MLF could, in the long run, have the same effect as its earlier obstruction of EDC—the creation of the national force the Soviet policy ostensibly was opposing.

and European disunity—and the two goals are seen by Moscow as interrelated. The Soviet leaders accordingly attach vital importance to gaining United States acceptance of the German division. Having failed during the second Berlin crisis in their direct effort to induce the West to recognize East Germany, they hope to achieve the same end by indirect means such as the proposed NATO-Warsaw Pact Nonaggression Treaty, which implicitly places East and West Germany on the same footing. To the extent that an American recognition of the East German regime would almost inevitably produce violent repercussions in Germany and strain the German-American alliance, it would be a contribution to new Western disunity. And as such, it would create a political situation pregnant with opportunities for Soviet diplomacy.

In time, the Soviet position may change and so may the Soviet definition of stability and security in Central Europe. The East European elites, in all probability never fully sharing in the great-power Russian ambitions and increasingly susceptible to their own peoples' desire for closer ties with the West, may exercise a salutary influence on the evolution of the Soviet attitude toward Europe. At present the East European margin for independent initiative in foreign policy is greatly limited by Soviet power, and this limit is further narrowed by their own fear of Germany. That fear is certainly greater in Prague or Warsaw than in Moscow, since neither Poland nor Czechoslovakia could resist alone a new German eastward expansion, and both entertain strong fears concerning the German attitude toward the existing frontiers. The overriding sense of dependence on the Soviet Union for protection against Germany inhibits any initiatives that deviate from Moscow's general line. It permits Moscow to preach eloquent neutralism to Scandinavia while forcibly denying any political validity for neutralism in East Europe.[17]

As a result, initiatives such as the Rapacki Plan, or its later refinement named after Gomulka, while presumably derived from the genuine Polish interest in safeguarding Central European security, still aimed their political sharp edge at

West Germany, implicitly postulating acceptance by the West of parity between the West and East German states. The Polish proposals also ignored the degree to which West Europe was disturbed by the concentration of Soviet MRBM's on Soviet western frontiers. On June 18, 1964, in response to a West German inquiry, the Poles made it clear that the Gomulka proposal for a nuclear weapons freeze did not include the USSR. In effect, the Polish proposal meant a freeze on further American security measures in Europe (since Germany is the principal locus of American forces), with the Soviet Union remaining immune to such restrictions.

It is a hopeful sign that, in spite of this persisting political bias, some East European states (as already noted in the earlier chapters) have displayed a more independent judgment concerning such multilateral western institutions as EEC and GATT. Greater realism in economics eventually may spread to politics as well. In late 1964 some East European leaders began to indicate an interest in the workings of the technical arms of the Council of Europe, and it is to be expected that such contacts will eventually spill over into the political areas. This is bound to stimulate a further sense of European identity among the East Europeans and thus to decrease the sense of dependence on Moscow. Since the East European elites are still presumably anxious to maintain their relationship with Moscow and, whenever relevant, to obtain the advantages of Soviet protection, they will be likely to advise Moscow to reassess its general commitment to a policy predicated on the desirability and inevitability of West European fragmentation.

Soviet receptivity to this advice—and hence its willingness to abandon the expectation of a decisive success on "the central front"—is likely to be conditioned both by the internal evolution of Soviet society (see Chapter I, sect. 4) and, even more important, by the stability of the international situation. The Soviet Union has acted as a revolutionary power whenever the international system crumbled and created vacuums that could be filled by communist power, or whenever the Soviet leaders assumed that they had superior power at their disposal. The gradual "europeanization" of Russia, the changing character of the Soviet stake in East Europe, and, above all, stability in the West, are likely to induce in the Soviet leaders, in a cumulative and mutually reinforcing fashion, an eventual willingness to reexamine Russia's relationship to Europe. Such a change would be made easier if, in the meantime, Western policies also promoted evolutionary changes in the relations between the two halves of Europe, so that the long awaited "settlement," when it came, would seem to involve merely the creative act of recognizing new realities. At that point Moscow might have no choice but to reconcile itself to the fact that Europe is not a place where communist history is still to be written.

Germany and East Europe

Stability in Europe is not possible as long as a leading European nation has one-fourth of its people under foreign domination and as long as half of European civilization is artificially cordoned off from the rest. The very existence of this condition breeds pressure for change, a predisposition to launch a sudden crisis, and a reciprocal and self-feeding desire for the accumulation of military power, either to change or to defend this division.

At the present the Soviet Union can count on the Poles and the Czechs for solid support for its policy of maintaining the division of Germany. The official East European attitude is succinctly defined in the resolution of the Fourth Congress of the Polish Communist Party held in June 1964: "It is not the division of Germany into two states with different social systems which is the source of tension and a threat of war in Europe." The statement went on to assert that, while "the German problem still remains the greatest obstacle to a relaxation of tensions and the peaceful settlement of international relations," the real cause of tensions is West German policy. In the official Warsaw view, the only way to stabilize Europe is for the West to recognize the existence of the two German states.

The Polish view, supported by the Czechs, links communist and nationalist interests. Some communist elites subscribe to Moscow's commitment to East Germany and perhaps even share some of the more aggressive purposes of the communist presence in the heart of Europe. The peoples have a simpler and more basic concern: they fear that a reunited Germany would seek to alter the present Polish and Czech frontiers. To the Poles particularly this is a matter of life and death: having lost half of their territory to the Russians, having been devastated and massacred by both the Germans and the Russians, having moved and settled some eight million people on the territories assigned to them by the Potsdam agreement (which also provided for the expulsion of the Germans from the said territories), and having rebuilt the new territories into an essential component of their economy, any threat to their territorial integrity not only reawakens all the memories of the Nazi occupation but poses the prospect of national extinction.* In that context, it is not too difficult for the Polish government to make East Germany appear as an essential buffer guaranteeing Polish security, and a Polish-Soviet alliance as the sine qua non of continued national survival. On that even anticommunists and communists agree.[18]

Western and particularly German policy has helped the communists in fostering this unity between communism and nationalism. Until approximately the end of the Eisenhower-Dulles period, Western policy on the German question was largely shaped by a defensive preoccupation with assuring

---

* Before the war, these territories amounted to 21.4% of German territory, were inhabited by 13.8% of the German population, and accounted for 6.3% of the German industrial production. For Poland in 1964, these figures were 32.4%, 26%, and approximately 25% respectively. For a fuller and objective analysis of the vital economic importance of these territories for Poland, see Georg Bluhm, *Die Oder-Neisse Linie in der Deutschen Aussenpolitik*, 1963.

NATO security, and it was formulated primarily by Washington in collaboration with Bonn. The basic failure of this policy was its fundamental assumption that some day there would be a formal East-West settlement providing for German reunification, and that prior to that settlement nothing should be conceded to the other side. Doubtless, some Germans entertained the hope that such a settlement would lead simultaneously or subsequently to a revision of the Oder-Neisse frontier, but even those who recognized its finality also held that renunciation of the territory east of the Oder-Neisse was a diplomatic asset to be saved until it could be traded advantageously in the course of such settlement.

This position was reinforced by the legal consideration that the Potsdam agreement, establishing the Oder-Neisse frontier and providing for the total expulsion of the Germans living east of it, did contain the formal stipulation that the final acknowledgment of this boundary would await the German peace treaty. It is now easy to see in retrospect how this reservation was gradually transformed in the course of the cold war into a major argument against the recognition of the frontier prior to a peace treaty. Perhaps in 1949 it might have been possible for the Western powers to exact from the newly constituted Federal German government its acknowledgment of the territorial changes effected in 1945; but at that time, with the cold war at its peak, there seemed little point in doing so, and many feared that the Russians would exploit any allied pressure on the new West German government to fan anti-NATO sentiments in West Germany. The only concession to East European fears was a declaration issued by the West German government in October 1954 that it would not rely on force to achieve either reunification or a revision of its frontiers. This, however, also implied the continued German desire to change the frontiers. In the meantime in Germany opposition to the frontier had time to organize an active constituency, the 10 million-odd expellees from all of East Europe, and the formal German position that the 1937 frontiers of Germany are still valid gradually jelled. Although not making a formal claim to the Sudetenland, the West German position on the Czech frontier was somewhat ambivalent, with the West Germans not renouncing until 1964 the Munich agreements.

Germany thus came to be committed to two mutually incompatible goals: reunification and frontier revision. While the latter was posited more by implication and many Germans privately conceded that they no longer expected any change in the Oder-Neisse boundary, the very linkage of the two tended to reinforce the East European stake in keeping Germany divided, and in turn linked East European communism and nationalism together.* The insistence of the West German government on the proposition that the only legal frontiers of Germany are those of 1937 was all the more incongruous in view of the growing German recognition that the unification of Germany depended on evolutionary changes in the communist world—that German unity would be achieved by a process of change and not by a formal settlement. The settlement, when and if it took place, would merely ratify changes effected in the meantime by evolution. Hence anything which impeded the process impeded German reunification. A real act of statesmanship required a clear perception of what stood in the way. Seen in that light, West German nonrecognition of the Oder-Neisse line was far from being an asset, "a trump card" to be played at the long awaited green table; nonrecognition was a Soviet asset that could only be negated by the West Germans themselves.

For a long time, however, as a thoughtful German com-

---

* The tendency for the Western powers to be drawn into this self-defeating contradiction was illustrated by the statement issued on June 26, 1964, by the United States, France, and the United Kingdom, in consultation with Bonn, in reaction to the "Treaty of Friendship" concluded between the Soviet Union and East Germany. The statement rejected the communist charges concerning West German "revanchism" by asserting: "The Government of the Federal Republic in its statement of October 3rd, 1954, has renounced the use of force to achieve the reunification of Germany or the modification of the present boundaries of the Federal Republic of Germany. This remains its policy." The East Europeans could hardly draw any comfort from the thought that a "modification of the present boundaries," albeit executed peacefully, remained the policy of one of the principal NATO powers. Actually, since the Oder-Neisse line is not the present boundary of the Federal Republic, communist propaganda could argue that the assurance was not very meaningful.

mentator observed in the authoritative journal *Aussenpolitik,* German policy discouraged Poland and Czechoslovakia from favoring German reunification (and hence also eventual ties with the rest of Europe), almost as if determined to keep the Poles frightened and East Europe frozen.[19] The principal instruments of this negative policy were the Hallstein doctrine, designed initially to isolate the East German regime, and the insistence of the West Germans on the continued validity of the 1937 frontier. The Hallstein doctrine in many respects was justified. The only German government freely elected by three-fourths of the German people had every moral right to object to any nation which recognized a legal and political fiction imposed on one-fourth of its people by a foreign power. Doubtless the West German threat to sever relations with any state that recognized East Germany deterred many new states from extending their recognition to Ulbricht.

However, the West German government did make an exception for the USSR in 1955 on the grounds that the Soviet government was involved in German affairs. The West German unwillingness to make a similar provision for the East European states meant that only East Germany was represented in the East European capitals; until the appearance of the West German trade missions in the early sixties, the authentic voice of democratic Germany was not heard. Since a strong case could be made that it was not the threat of rupture in diplomatic relations but the West German capacity to extend (and hence to deny) economic aid to the new nations that deterred some of them from recognizing East Germany, the legalistic insistence on the application of the Hallstein doctrine to the East European states (which had already recognized East Germany) hurt only German interests.[20] Any subsequent initiation of diplomatic relations with the East European states could be represented by the communists as a breach in the Hallstein doctrine and hence as a precedent for others; continued insistence upon it put tortuous obstacles in the way of West German efforts to isolate East Germany by establishing contacts with East Europe.

Efforts to improve German-Polish relations, undertaken after the 1956 change in Poland, provide a classic example of the contradictions between the German realization of the German national interest in an improvement in relations with East Europe, and the German-erected obstacles to such an improvement; between the Polish national stake in better relations with Germany and the communist interest in retaining West Germany as the principal enemy, thereby intensifying the Polish sense of dependence on Soviet support. As soon as Poland had gained a margin of autonomy from Soviet control, it sought contacts with the West, although Gomulka was already using the German threat in his appeals for popular support for the Soviet-Polish alliance in the January 1957 "elections," a plebiscite to approve the October changes. In spite of this, the new Polish government expressed interest in the establishment of Polish-German diplomatic relations without requiring formal West German recognition of the new frontier.* But although the West German reaction to the new developments in Poland was genuinely sympathetic, the official response was negative, presumably because of the Hallstein doctrine. The Polish proposal was not accepted, and Dr. Heinrich von Brentano, the Foreign Minister, went so far as to assure the Poles, at a time when they were striving to increase their independence from Moscow, that the Polish-German frontier was "not acceptable now or in the future." [21]

For approximately a year, the Poles maintained their position that a resumption of diplomatic relations need not be dependent on the West German recognition of the Oder-Neisse frontier,[22] but subsequently their position stiffened, presumably because of the improvement in Polish-Soviet relations and

---

* The proposed formula was that each side would issue a declaration with its own interpretation of the territorial situation, on the model of the Soviet-West German arrangement of September 1955. See the interesting Polish account in K. Skubis-zewski, "Les Problèmes des relations diplomatiques entre la Pologne et la République Fédérale d'Allemagne," *Cahiers Pologne-Allemagne*, No. 4, October-November-December 1963. This version is not contradicted by a detailed and authoritative analysis by a German author, O. Stenzl, "Germany's Eastern Frontier," *Survey*, April 1964.

probably because Warsaw sensed a more widespread inclination in the West to accept the frontier. Warsaw accordingly
began to insist on a German recognition of the frontier as a
precondition for diplomatic relations. In the meantime, a partial but still very ambivalent change of heart had taken place
in Germany. In 1959, Chancellor Adenauer toyed with the
idea of offering a nonaggression pact to Poland and Czechoslovakia, but then dropped the notion in the face of violent
protests by the German Union of Expellees. A year earlier the
Social Democrats (SPD) and the Free Democrats (FDP) had
both proposed that Bonn enter into formal negotiations with
Warsaw concerning diplomatic relations, but under similar
pressure subsequently emasculated the proposal. Nonetheless,
a leading West German industrialist, Berthold Beitz, was sent
to Poland in 1960 and 1961 to explore Polish views. His efforts, however, were simultaneously undercut by belligerent
West German assertions, some by Adenauer himself, that the
former German territories should be and would be returned
to Germany, as well as by official German disavowals of his
mission.[23] It was not surprising that the Beitz mission failed.
His own view was that "the stupidity and ignorance manifested
by the members of the government in Bonn obstructed a German-Polish rapprochement." [24]

The passing of German foreign policy into the hands of
Chancellor Ludwig Erhard and Foreign Minister Gerhard
Schroeder came simultaneously with a shift in the American
attitude toward East Europe in the direction of developing
more extensive contacts (see below p. 118). Under the new
leadership Bonn strove to formulate an eastern policy that
could relate itself to the Eastern European evolution, and
overcome the legacy of the Hallstein doctrine and the frontier issue. The new German leaders had concluded apparently
that a formal settlement was not at hand. The reunification of
Germany would therefore depend in large measure on the
character of the future relations of Poland and Czechoslovakia, on the one hand, with Russia and Germany respectively

on the other, and West Germany would have a constructive role to play in shaping these relations.

The new German approach was formulated most fully in an extensive review of the world scene by Foreign Minister Gerhard Schroeder, delivered on April 3, 1964.[25] While the speech reasserted the central German concern with reunification, it was notable for its emphasis on the evolutionary changes in East Europe and for its tone of moderation and sympathy with regard to the divisive issue of the Polish-German frontier. Reiterating the formal German position that "the final course of the German frontier should be determined peacefully and without any use of force in a peace treaty with the whole of Germany," the Foreign Minister went on to assure the Poles that "we do not want to open old wounds" and appealed for the normalization of relations. He concluded his remarks on East Europe with a passage that spelled out the significantly novel assumptions guiding German policy:

"We do not expect our Eastern European policy to yield any spectacular success. But if we continue to steer our course patiently and consistently we will promote understanding for our position in East Europe, too. The Poles, for instance, in particular should be well able to place themselves in our position, for they know from their own history that a nation cannot remain divided for ever. I believe there are indications that in some East European countries there is growing understanding for the German problem and that their judgment is more independent than it has been in the past. It appears to me that our desire for true relaxation of tensions is meeting with more understanding in those countries than with the Soviet government for the time being. Let us not underrate this trend, for the voice of those states is beginning to carry more weight."

In keeping with this general approach,[26] the West Germans indicated their willingness to grant five-year credits to East Europe and to expand cultural contacts. With the United States as intermediary, they also sought to settle their disagreements with Yugoslavia.

In its essence, the West German effort to improve relations with East Europe was an attempt to ignore the difficult issue of the Oder-Neisse frontier while normalizing other relationships. However, to the extent that Moscow in particular and the communists in general have a vested interest in maintaining an abyss between West Germany and East Europe, German inability to face squarely the frontier issue gave the other side a convenient opportunity to deflect and emasculate the new German efforts. They were simply represented to the East Europeans as involving a devious two-stage approach: during the first stage, West Germany and the United States would be seeking to sever the East European states from the Soviet Union so that they could compel the reunification of Germany; in the second stage, a unified and powerful Germany would have a free hand in dealing with isolated Poland and Czechoslovakia.

The East Germans especially made no secret of the fact that they saw in West German contacts with East Europe a threat to communism: "Schroeder thinks that the exchange of official trade missions between West Germany and some people's democracies is a particularly cunning move. Its aim is to restore active contacts by the Bonn Government which had isolated itself from the majority of socialist countries by its Hallstein Doctrine and its demand for revision of the existing borders. Connected with it is the illusion of being able to weaken the close relations of the GDR with some people's democracies, first by economic and later by other means. . . . Thus Schroeder hopes eventually to establish de facto diplomatic relations with the people's democracies without officially abandoning his Hallstein Doctrine. He regards it as a special merit for himself that in this way he avoids official recognition of the borders which would be included in the establishment of normal diplomatic relations. In other words, this policy of exchanging trade missions is meant to help the Bonn government escape from the self-created cage of the Hallstein Doctrine and to keep its hands free to pursue a revanchist policy." [27]

Also symptomatic was the reaction of the Czech communist government to German efforts to assuage Czech fears. In the summer of 1964 a West German cabinet member, Dr. Hans Seebohm, provoked a public outcry throughout the West by insisting that the Munich pact was still valid. In response, the West German Chancellor, Ludwig Erhard, explicitly declared on June 11, 1964, in a speech delivered before the New York Council on Foreign Relations, that the agreement "was torn to pieces by Hitler" and that Germany "has no territorial claims whatsoever with regard to Czechoslovakia and separates itself expressly from any declarations which have given rise to a different interpretation." Nonetheless, ten days later the Czech Foreign Minister, V. David, addressing a mass rally, appealed to the anti-German sentiments and fears of the masses by asserting that "The German Federal Republic is not only refusing to draw legal and political conclusions from the nonvalidity of the Munich diktat, but actually is avoiding explicit nonrecognition of this nonvalidity." [28] Similarly, the Polish communist celebrations of the twentieth anniversary of communist power in Poland were dominated by an anti-German theme, with West German rearmament (including the MLF) and the frontier issue paramount.

This extremely negative and hostile communist response was encouraged by the somewhat contradictory attitude of the West German government itself toward the frontier issue, in spite of the general thrust of Schroeder's policy statement. In a note addressed to Khrushchev on February 26, 1964, a month prior to Schroeder's address, Chancellor Erhard seemed to confirm the "two stages" charge by noting that he was "convinced that after the formation of an all-German government it will also be possible to arrive at an equitable settlement of the German eastern frontier, giving due consideration to the peoples affected."

In his March 16, 1964, "interim report" on the international situation, the Chancellor described the present frontier as a creation of Stalin, designed to divide Germans and Poles, adding "We want to talk to our eastern neighbors about this";

speaking a week later to the Congress of the German Expellees, he asserted that Germany cannot renounce its "rights"
to these territories and stressed the principle of "the right to
homeland" of the German expellees.* Two weeks after
Schroeder's address, the West German government, com-
menting on a Polish-Soviet communique asserting the finality
of the Oder-Neisse frontier, noted that the boundary issue
would remain unsettled until the peace treaty. Even in the
New York speech of June 11, 1964, notable for its renunciation
of the Munich pact and for the implied criticism of the West
German cabinet minister who held that it was still valid,† the
Chancellor invoked the injustices involved in the expulsion
more than 20 years ago of the Germans from the territories
east of the present frontier, again maintained that the frontier
was a plot by Stalin, and asserted that the frontier can only
be "established" after German reunification.‡ In effect, the
West German government seemed to be inviting the Poles
and the Czechs to assist in the reunification of Germany
with the prospect of subsequently having to face Germany
alone.¶

* "The right to homeland" could become a double edged sword, since it is bound
to lapse with the passage of time. A. von Schack in "Heimatrecht and Self-
Determination," *Aussenpolitik*, June 1964, criticizes the concept, noting that, with
the death of the German expellees and the births among the Polish settlers, there
would soon be more Poles enjoying "the right of homeland." For some data on
the number of refugees actually willing to resettle in their old homes, see Stenzl,
op. cit., p. 128. He states that only 7% were definitely desirous of returning.
† Dr. Hans Seebohm, the Minister of Transport, active in the expellee movement,
was nonetheless retained in the cabinet, a matter fully exploited by Czech and
Polish propagandists.
‡ For a long review of a variety of other incidents that provide grist for the
communist opponents of the German-Polish rapprochement, see Stenzl, *op. cit.*
These range from the use in German television of meteorological maps that
include one-third of Poland to political attacks in Germany on German intellectuals who have recommended an acceptance of the Oder-Neisse frontier,
including demands by some West German politicians that they be sentenced to
prison. Stenzl is a staff member of the *Forschungsinstitut der Deutschen Gesell-
schaft fur Auswärtige Politik* in Bonn.
¶ This is also the sense of the advice offered the Poles by D. S. Collier and K.
Glazer, *Berlin and the Future of East Europe*, Chicago, 1963, p. 19, who urged
the Poles to assist German reunification while on the frontier issue they should
now "agree to disagree." The same impression is generated by the approach taken
by the SPD foreign affairs expert, F. Erler, in his "Les Aspects politiques de
l'action sovietique à Berlin," *Politique Étrangère*, No. 1, 1962, p. 11.

Although relations did gradually improve with some of the other East European states, German freedom of movement with regard to Poland, the key area to German reunification, thus has been shackled by the ambivalence of the official policy on the crucial frontier issue. Moreover, the formation of a more active German eastern policy, free of the *immobilisme* induced by the Hallstein doctrine and by the seeming formal commitment to revisionism on the frontier issue, was complicated by domestic factors. Although the refugee party had faded and German public opinion polls illustrated the declining importance of the territorial issue, the absorption by the major parties of the former refugee votes, making them the swing vote between two rather evenly matched parties, made even the SPD more rigid on the frontier issue.

Furthermore, the emerging Schroeder strategy of forward movement toward East Europe has been challenged on two fronts: on the left by those who advocate the extension of his policy to include East Germany and perhaps even to seek a solution by developing a special relationship with Moscow, and on the right by those who objected to the policy on general grounds, and who on issues pertaining to the Western alliance favored a pro-De Gaulle orientation. Both sides reflect a mounting feeling of frustration in Germany over the continued division of the country and testify indirectly to the failure of West Germany, unwilling to separate that issue from the frontier problem, to find an effective way to undo its partition.*

The feeling of frustration expressed itself at one extreme of the foreign policy spectrum by the willingness of the Berlin mayor and SPD leader, Willy Brandt, to seek considerably more contact with East Germany even at the risk of somewhat enhancing through indirect arrangements the formal status of the East German regime. The argument advanced in favor of this position was that anything that brings the

---

* German public opinion polls have shown an increase in German concern over the problem of unification and the number of those who stated that they were "beginning to get used to" the division decreasing slightly from 33% in 1956 to 32% in 1963, despite the passage of the intervening seven years. For fuller accounts, see *The Bulletin*, December 10, 1963.

German people together brings also closer the day of reunification. The Free Democratic Party also formally favored the
Schroeder line, but some of its spokesmen even advocated a
review of West Germany's membership in NATO as a price
for reunification and expressed their willingness to deal bilaterally with the communist regime in East Germany, although without accepting the Oder-Neisse line.* Nonetheless,
their position with respect to East Germany and the Soviet
Union went beyond the limits considered desirable by the government and represented an altogether different alternative, in
some respects still wedded to the notion that the East German
problem can be extracted from the over-all question of East
Europe. Their posture fed Soviet hopes of eventual fragmentation of the West and on those grounds was rejected by Bonn.

The issue of Bonn's relations to East Germany posed an
especially complicated problem because of the emotional elements involved. Most West Germans shared in the desire
to alleviate the hardships experienced by the East Germans
and hoped for closer national contacts. Yet Schroeder seemed
justified in drawing a political distinction between East Germany and East Europe. Compromise on the formerly rigid
stand of the Hallstein doctrine, and perhaps eventually on the
frontier issue, would make closer relations with East Europe
possible and hence could eventually contribute to reunification,
but compromise on the firm definition of the East German
regime as a tool of the Soviet occupation forces could contribute to the perpetuation of that regime. Indeed, even a
case could be made against policies designed to moderate its

* See the remarks by T. Dehler, W. Scheel (a Minister in the cabinet) and E.
Achenbach at the 1964 FDP Duisburg convention. Also the interview with Erich
Mende, the FDP leader, *Die Zeit*, January 24, 1964, supporting the view that East
Germany may be liberalized. On FDP approval of the Brandt 1963 Christmas
passes agreement in Berlin, see *Freie Demokratische Correspondenz*, February 21,
1964. (Politically isolated but prominent intellectuals, such as Karl Jaspers, Golo
Mann, and the authors of the Tübingen memorandum have advocated acceptance
of the frontier, but their direct political influence appears limited. For an extreme
statement favoring the recognition of Ulbricht and a pullout from NATO as a
necessary price of reunification, see R. Schroers, "Is There a Movement for
Reunification?" *Merkur*, April 1962. For replies, the July issue).

internal character. Treating East Germany as the rest of East Europe could at best achieve an internal liberalization that might make the East German regime more palatable and respectable, but without diminishing its essential dependence on the Soviet Union. Communist East Germany, merely one-fourth of a country, could never become an internally self-sustaining regime like that of Gomulka or Gheorghiu-Dej; the inescapable attraction of West Germany would always be internally disruptive. Soviet support—and hence presence—would be constantly required. The new respectability and "moderation" would simply strengthen the hand of those in the West who already favor recognition. The division of Germany would thus have gained a formal sanction.

Alternatively, internal liberalization might encourage new public demands for unification. Eventually, the people might become emboldened by the decrease in coercion, with the danger of sudden eruptions. Soviet intervention would certainly follow, with disastrous effects for the East Germans. The net effect would be not only a threat to peace, but a setback for German reunification. The gradual isolation of East Germany seemed the wiser course, especially when undertaken in the context of improved relations with East Europe, provided the logjam on the Polish-German frontier issue could be broken.

Yet on that particular issue as well as with regard to the broad problem of German "Ostpolitik," Schroeder was faced with increasing opposition within his own party ranks. While personal rivalries were heavily involved, the issue expressed itself in disagreements over foreign policies. With regard to the broad issue of the European future, the opposition identified itself with Paris rather than Washington. It has been dubious about the MLF, even hinted at the desirability of German nuclear force, and—as an extension of the independent "European" conception—it advocated an essentially "hard" posture vis-à-vis the East. While accepting Schroeder's own opposition to any softening in the West German policy toward

East Germany, the opposition held that hopes for an East European evolution were ephemeral and the expectation that gradual changes can lead to reunification were a myth. It rejected any weakening in the German stand on the Oder-Neisse issue, on the grounds that since the East Europeans want to be liberated, anything which satisfies the demands of the governments weakens the peoples' spirit of resistance to Moscow and is therefore a pointless and even counterproductive concession. The importance of developments such as the Rumanian self-assertion or the Sino-Soviet dispute were held to have been vastly exaggerated and, in any case, were interpreted as offering no basis for Western optimism. In keeping with these general assumptions, specific moves, such as economic agreements or the Test Ban Treaty were explicitly rejected.*

In a nutshell, this alternative conception of German foreign policy, important because of its relation to Paris, subscribes to "the worse, the better" formula for the East. Its view of the East is that of a homogeneous, centrally orchestrated monolith, controlled from Moscow, with East Europe more of a threat to the West than the other way around.[29] Accordingly it rejects any effort to improve relations with the East, which it associates with the "soft" currents prevailing in Washington since 1961, and argues that only through sustained pressure on the East and the simultaneous creation of a powerful Europe can the West attain its objectives.[30]

It is doubtful, however, that the alternative policy can be more successful. It certainly ignores East European realities and opportunities, which Schroeder has perceived, and the changes that have taken place even in the French attitude toward East Europe (see next section). It rests on the assumption that a policy of pressure and isolation would somehow prompt the entire communist structure to dissolve (a view

---

* E. g., Georg von Huebbenet, in "Can Economic Aid Soften Up the East Bloc?", *Aussenpolitik*, November 1962, advocates the economic isolation of the East and argues that Tito's and Gomulka's claims of independence are fraudulently designed to qualify for U.S. aid.

finally disowned by Dulles in 1957), or, if the dissolution should take place in an individual communist state, that the Soviet Union would not be able to restore the status quo ante (as in Hungary in 1956). It takes comfort in the short-range notion that denial of economic aid to individual communist states, even those that have asserted some autonomy of Moscow, will contribute to the over-all economic difficulties of the bloc, disregarding the high probability that without the Western option the long-range gainer will be CEMA, with the Soviet-advocated program of tighter economic (and hence political) integration. Finally, by ignoring the reality of Polish and Czech—and even Russian—fears of a rearmed and self-assertive Germany and by being inclined even to take advantage of the opportunistic Chinese territorial gambits,* it reconsolidates in East Europe the union of communism and nationalism to the detriment of the cause of German reunification.

To be effective in dispelling Soviet offensive hopes and in attaining the goal of unification, German policy must conclusively refute any Soviet expectations of separating Germany from the West and must strive to convince the Soviet Union that its control over East Germany is inevitably doomed by the thrust of European, including East European, developments. A "soft" policy risks rekindling the Soviet hope of fragmenting the West while even gaining Western recognition for the East German regime. A "hard" policy, on the other hand, would weaken German-American ties, and drive East Europe into a closer relationship with the Soviet Union, thereby cementing

---

* Mao Tse-tung's revival in the summer of 1964 of the various European territorial disputes, including the matter of the 1945 Russian and Polish acquisition of formerly German territories, was explicitly welcomed by these elements as providing a new lodestar for German policy. In a front-page lead article, *Der Rheinische Merkur* rhapsodized over Mao Tse-tung's statement as an attack on the Soviet-American partnership for the preservation of the Potsdam agreement and concluded by stating that Bonn should try to win over its Western allies to an acceptance of these theses of Mao. P. W. Wenger, "Peking's Potsdam Attacks Should Be Utilized," *Der Rheinische Merkur* (editorial), September 11, 1964. Previously, these same circles had dismissed the Sino-Soviet dispute as unimportant.

the Soviet position on the Elbe. The Schroeder line comes closest to facing reality but its inability to break with the legacy of the Hallstein doctrine and with the formal position on the Oder-Neisse line, provides the communist side with advantageous weapons for reducing its effectiveness. Caught in the web of domestic politics and conflicting national strategies, with its eastern vision still restricted by narrow national perspectives, Germany, unless prompted by some external inspiration, is still not able to take the necessary steps for undermining its own and the European partition.

France and Europe to the Urals

De Gaulle has been the most articulate and the most visionary critic of the European partition. "Let us build Europe," he would cry out, evoking the memory of Charlemagne, as he appealed to the "Gaullic, Germanic, and Latin peoples" to join in constructing a "European Europe," that is, one free both of American and Russian influence.[31] Taking the new European sense of confidence and security as his point of departure, he has pressed steadily to diminish American political influence on the continent, hoping to replace it by Franco-German concord.

Given the limits imposed on German rearmament and, more important, the moral and political factors involved, De Gaulle could reasonably assume that the political (and perhaps also military) leadership in that relationship would inevitably be exercised by France. To assure that end, and also to increase Europe's influence on American military policy (at least to the point of achieving the capacity to involve the United States even against its desire), he undertook to transform France into a nuclear power. The long-range importance of this more than compensated, in his view, for the temporary isolation and even unpopularity of France. Only thus could he defeat the Anglo-Saxon conception of an Atlantic community in which, as he saw it, the political and military power would be controlled almost entirely from Washington and London. A tightly integrated Western Europe subject to such "external" control would be, as he put it on September 28, 1963, a Europe "without a soul, without backbone, and without roots," subject "to one or the other of the two foreign hegemonies." [32]

In De Gaulle's view, such a Europe would become the tool of the two superpowers, the U.S.A. and the USSR, whose interests in Europe were no longer incompatible. Moscow, it would seem, no longer expected to be able to swallow up (in the near future, at least) the rest of Europe, and was content to remain on the Elbe, busy consolidating its rear. America, despite what its leaders said, accepted that division. De Gaulle expressed this view on July 29, 1963: "The United States, which since Yalta and Potsdam has had nothing to demand from the Soviets, now sees prospects of understanding opening before it. The result is the separate negotiations between the Anglo-Saxons and the Soviets, which, starting from the restricted nuclear test agreement, appear about to be extended to other questions, notably European questions, and so far in the absence of any Europeans. This obviously runs counter to the views of France." [33] Having held America responsible for the division of Europe, De Gaulle then asserted that in time "a complete change in the relations between East and West in Europe" would become possible and that "when this day comes, and I have said this before, France expects to make constructive proposals concerning the peace, equilibrium, and destiny of Europe."

De Gaulle and his associates have given several hints as to what these "constructive proposals" might be. Seeing Central Europe as "vital" and as "a question of life and death" to West Europe,[34] a feeling seemingly not shared by America, and noting the continued importance of the role of "the personality and responsibility of States" in international affairs,[35] the French argued that the basic reality in Europe was not the cold war but the fact that "the old division . . . is outmoded." [36] Hopeful that East Europe "will gradually come to an evolution compatible with our own transformation" (i.e., West European independence of America),[37] De Gaulle's vision saw the eventual absorption of East Europe and Russia in a larger European community, based on a common cultural and historical heritage and defined geographically in a speech by the French leader on March 25, 1959. In that speech he developed the theme of "Europe to the Urals," linking it to an eloquent plea for a common sense of European enterprise:

"We, who live between the Atlantic and the Urals, we, who are Europe, possessing with Europe's daughter, America, the principal sources and resources of civilization . . . why do we not pool a percentage of our raw materials, our manufactured goods, our food products, some of our scientists, technologists, economists, some of our trucks, ships and aircraft in order to vanquish misery, develop the resources, and the trust in work, of less developed peoples? Let us do this not that they should be the pawns of our policies, but to improve the chances of life and peace. How much more worthwhile that would be than the territorial demands, ideological claims, imperialist ambitions which are leading the world to its death!" [38]

Since then De Gaulle has frequently alluded to this concept. Thus on May 31, 1960, "taking into account the probable evolution of political regimes," he envisioned "a European entente from the Atlantic to the Urals" and on May 15, 1962, he even more explicitly made the Franco-German entente a condition on which depends "the destiny of the whole of Europe from the Atlantic to the Ural mountains: for if a structure, a firm, prosperous and attractive organization can be created in Western Europe—then there reappear the possibilities of a European balance with the Eastern states and the prospect of a truly European cooperation, particularly if, at the same time, the totalitarian regimes cease to poison the springs." *

---

* Reynaud, *op. cit.*, pp. 22–25 shows that "Europe to the Urals" has been a persistent Gaullist theme since at least the end of World War II.

De Gaulle sees this emerging as the culmination of a lengthy process of transformation within the communist states, perhaps accelerated by the Sino-Soviet conflict and the growing attraction of Europe and the Common Market.* Accordingly, De Gaulle, who has frequently alluded to the importance of the Sino-Soviet border dispute, has cultivated China, hoping that Russia's new sense of encirclement might even make her more anxious to become part of Europe. Eventually, according to a long-range and optimistic projection by one of De Gaulle's admirers,[39] the "European" Europe would be able to propose to the Soviet Union a new solution for liquidating the division of Europe and provide an alternative to the Soviet-American international system. According to this version, Russian troops would withdraw from East Germany and all European satellites, with priority given to the closest neighbors of the economic community, that is to say, Poland, Czechoslovakia, and Hungary. These countries would regain a free exercise of national sovereignty and would be able to associate with Europe economically and even politically. The Atlantic Pact and the Warsaw Treaty would be dissolved. American troops would leave Europe and the European community together with Russia would engage in large-scale economic development.

The power of De Gaulle's vision was not matched by the power of his means. Yet this he did not consider necessarily a fatal liability. Although recognizing the continued vital importance to European security of American military power and hence repeatedly stressing the defensive value of the alliance with America, to build "a European Europe" De Gaulle purposely excluded American power. To him this was both essential and convenient: essential, for otherwise Europe

* Some Gaullist spokesmen have projected this process even further. See Jacques de Montalais, *Le Monde*, August 22, 1962, who sees the following outcome: "Europe extended southward through Africa and eastward through Siberia; the United States extended northward through Canada and southward through Latin America; and finally China . . . ," in effect a world demarcated geographically by several major regional or continental powers—Europe and Russia, China, America, and the Western Hemisphere.

would remain the appendage of America; convenient, because that American power checkmated Soviet power, and permitted France to rely on maneuver and deception in seeking a grand policy without great power.

Both maneuver and deception were essential, for in many respects De Gaulle was seeking, at least in the short run, contradictory goals. He had to gain West German friendship and loyalty to his scheme while simultaneously diluting the East European, and even Russian, fears of the Germans. In spite of De Gaulle's close ties with Germany, which he sees as the backbone for independent European action, he has hoped gradually to accelerate the process of amalgamating Russia into Europe by lessening the fear of the East Europeans of a renewed German "Drang nach Osten." In this connection he has gone further than Washington. He has seen that acceptance of the present Polish-German frontier on the Oder-Neisse Rivers as permanent is the sine qua non for drawing Poland back into the European orbit.* And obviously, given the geographic location of Poland and its present links with Russia, Poland would be the vital link in any eventual return of Russia to a European orientation.

De Gaulle's preoccupation with East Europe reveals the strong element of *sacro egoismo* and deception in his policy. Since his concept of Europe is one led by France, it follows that the two alternatives for France are 1) Europe divided on the Elbe, in which a divided Germany depends on France for eventual reunification, or 2) a united Europe including not only a

---

* De Gaulle said in his press conference, March 25, 1959: "The reunification of the two parts into a single Germany which would be entirely free seems to us the normal destiny of the German people, *provided they do not reopen the question of their present frontiers to the west, the east, the north, and the south,* and that they move toward integrating themselves one day in a contractual organization of all Europe for cooperation, liberty and peace." (Italics added.) On November 10, 1959, asked specifically about the Oder-Neisse frontier, he replied: "I said in a similar conference what I think about the question you just asked . . . you need only know that I have not changed my mind." Premier M. Debré in a statement to the National Assembly of October 19, 1959, reiterated that West German respect for the existing boundaries "including the so-called Oder-Neisse line" is a basic condition for German reunification.

70-million-strong Germany but also East Europe (and even Russia), for the latter combined with France would more than balance Germany. He therefore could not welcome a re-unification of Germany while East Europe remained in the hands of a hostile and perhaps fearful Russia. Accordingly, he even dampened German hopes for reunification: "I repeat, in the light of the extremely precarious balance that exists be-tween the East and the West, our view on Germany is that it is not opportune, at the present time, to alter the facts that have already been accomplished there. We believe that these facts should be taken as they are and lived with." [40]

To balance any German resentment, he has taken ad-vantage of the present American policy. The United States implicitly accepts the division on the Elbe while explicitly preaching reunification, leaving the eastern frontiers of Ger-many undefined and thus giving the Poles no alternative but to support Moscow and Pankow wholeheartedly. De Gaulle has verbally adopted a more militant stand. He refused to par-ticipate in the American-Soviet talks on Berlin and was the only top Western leader to warn publicly of possible sanctions against Soviet ships and planes on the high seas and in the skies, should the Soviets interfere with Western access (Sep-tember 5, 1961). He categorically and uncompromisingly re-jected the Soviet proposal for a NATO-Warsaw Treaty Non-aggression Pact and rejected any idea of equivalence between the Atlantic alliance and "communist servitude."

Indeed for the time being, German *immobilisme* on the subject of frontiers, together with the Hallstein doctrine and American tolerance of the division of Europe, were all in keeping with De Gaulle's wishes: since it was too early to move in the East, Franco-German political unity in the West should be forged meanwhile at the expense of "passive" Amer-ica. If the United States and Germany were to move first in recognizing the Oder-Neisse line and attempting political-economic penetration of East Europe, France would be found unprepared and unable to exercise leadership. But in time,

De Gaulle believed, Germany would come to realize the futility of the American approach to its problems;* then the moment would be ripe for France to seek actively a "Europe to the Urals." (Could the exclusion of the Soviet realm beyond the Urals be an appeal to the Chinese?)

While pursuing the "European Europe" as a necessary springboard for an offensive Eastern policy, De Gaulle has been careful to keep open his doors to the East. This was important not only to the eventual success of his policy which required a gradual lessening in East European tensions; it also provided him with subtle means for inducing the Germans to follow France out of fear lest France seek some accommodation with Russia on the basis of the European status quo. The Eastern option could also be the source of an alternative policy in the event that the Paris-Bonn axis is ruptured. In many respects, Russia had more to offer to France than to Germany. At the very least, the Germans could purchase reunification at the cost of the exclusion of America from Germany and German dependence on Russia; at the worse, at the cost of communization of the whole of Germany. Hence the Russian offer could not be very attractive. Yet De Gaulle might calculate that a Franco-Russian concord could have as its object the elimination of American influence from Europe, the effect of it being not the establishment of Russian domination, but an acceleration in the process of Western European federation under the aegis of France and as an independent counterweight to Russia. In the context of a divided Europe and a partitioned Germany, a Franco-Soviet "Rapallo" was more meaningful than a Russo-German one.

But even short of such a dramatic *dénouement* in the configuration of European politics, French flexibility toward the East was essential to the realization of De Gaulle's long-

---

* To perceive that this is not entirely unrealistic one should remind oneself of the Strauss and von Guttenberg alternative to the Schroeder line. See also the two articles in the German publication *Aussenpolitik* by the French military expert, Ferdinand Miksche, "Should the Western Powers Negotiate with the East?" (August and September 1962), highly critical of the American posture.

range vision. French flexibility necessarily rose in importance as the post-Adenauer-Erhard regime began to reassert the primacy of the German-American tie, and as Schroeder's new German line, executed in correspondence with the United States, posed the risk of the East European initiative being preempted by Washington and Bonn, with France isolated on the sidelines.

Accordingly, Paris activated its own policies in East Europe, notwithstanding De Gaulle's earlier condemnation of the East European regimes as "fraudulent intermediaries of Russia" and his hope that the East European initiative might have been made jointly by France and Germany. (In his press conference of July 23, 1964, De Gaulle spoke with a touch of sadness about joint French and West German initiatives, including on the subject of frontiers, that might have been made had Bonn only followed his lead.) The intensified French contacts with Soviet statesmen, the exchanges and trade with the communist states, and finally the much publicized French-Rumanian cooperation agreement, initialed in July 1964, after a personal call on De Gaulle by the Rumanian Prime Minister, indicated growing French involvement in East Europe. At the same time certain ambiguous gestures toward East Germany might have been meant as pointed warning signals to Bonn.* Indeed, the more the Franco-German alliance floundered, the more active French contacts with East Europe and Russia were likely to become.

The vision of a Europe stretching to the Urals was captivating and grandiose. Moreover, and this explained much of its appeal even among De Gaulle's European critics, it seemed to be in keeping with the thrust of European development. There was no doubt that he alone among the Western states-

---

* The Germans were particularly concerned by the visit early in 1964 to the East German regime, including conferences with Ulbricht, of a number of French deputies, including five from De Gaulle's own party. Subsequently, the French government violated NATO agreements and granted special permission for a German Communist Party delegation to attend the funeral of Thorez. The French government has also not obstructed the "twinning" of the cities of Lille and Erfurt in East Germany.

men had conceived and articulated a tomorrow for Europe that seemed to have more substance than either the vague American talk about "a world safe for diversity" or the crude boastings of Khrushchev about "burying" the noncommunist way of life. Furthermore, East Europe in particular, with the renewed emphasis on the supremacy of the nation-state, with the fears of supranational organs—whether CEMA or the EEC—, seemed particularly ripe terrain for the Gaullist vision of a Europe of states. To the East European national communists the ideal solution might well seem to be that advocated by De Gaulle: a Europe of nationalist (and in some cases also communist) states, with Russian fears of such a Europe diminished by the expulsion of American influence from the continent.

Yet basically De Gaulle's policies—even if not his ultimate image of the shape of things to come—were contradictory and self-defeating. Having a clear goal is not the same thing as having a policy—although only too often his critics (especially in the United States) had instead a policy but no goals. The gap between French ends and means, preventing France from using economic or military power to pressure allies or to purchase friends, dictated not only a policy of sudden maneuver (for example, the exclusion of Great Britain from the Common Market) but also a posture of obstinate insistence on its point of view. As a result, the French President, in his press conference of July 23, 1964, had to list among the opponents of his concept of Europe no less than five leading European capitals (Bonn, Rome, The Hague, Brussels, not to speak of London), in addition to the established *bête noire,* Washington. "Splendid isolation" was a mocking term often applied in the past to describe England in relation to the Continent. France's isolated grandeur seemed hardly an auspicious point of departure toward "European Europe."

French nuclear policy also contributed to the isolation of France. Leaving aside its military aspects,[41] the political case for it seemed contradictory. General de Gaulle stressed the importance of an independent French nuclear deterrent on the grounds that no self-respecting nation could depend on another for its survival. But if that was the case, then the only logical conclusion was for each European nation to seek its own nuclear arsenal, for surely there was no reason to rely for protection on a weak and technologically doubtful French force when a much more comprehensive and impregnable American deterrent was available. Paris gave no hint that eventually the French force would be transformed into a European one, subject to some still undefined European control. On the contrary, all the French comments, projecting the state of the force into the seventies, made it clear that French control was not going to lapse. Consequently, there was little inclination on the Continent to provide material support for the French nuclear development. French hints that France would welcome German technical and especially fiscal assistance fell on deaf ears. As "Sirius" noted in *Le Monde,* "Once again, the argumentation of General de Gaulle turns against him and ruins his own designs." [42]

The French efforts to undercut the American position in Europe, furthermore, hurt the tenderly developed Franco-German relationship. To the Germans, continued and stable United States presence in Central Europe was a sine qua non of their security. No German could expect West Berlin to remain free without the American presence and without, above all, the American willingness to fight. There was simply no substitute for this, and although De Gaulle continued stressing the high value that France attached to the *defensive* NATO alliance, the Germans were concerned that the political effect of De Gaulle's policies would be an eventual reexamination of the American commitment. They feared that this reexamination would not take place according to De Gaulle's own personal timetable, i.e., when France and the "European Europe" were fully able to shoulder the military burden, but much earlier—and that Germany would be the first to feel the pinch.

The Germans could be—and were—sympathetic to De Gaulle's seemingly harder line on the Berlin issue; they saw in the Bonn-Paris axis a useful lever for hardening the American posture, but certainly not a mechanism for reducing their own reliance on American protection nor an instrument for promoting the European fragmentation, so long awaited by the Soviets.

German enthusiasm for De Gaulle has also been diminished by De Gaulle's own "opening to the East." The courtship of East Europe, exemplified by the French-Rumanian agreement, the ambiguous gestures toward East Germany, and the potential flirtation with Russia were all in direct conflict with the "hard" Eastern policy recommended by De Gaulle's German admirers, and undercut their own opposition to Schroeder. They could forgive De Gaulle's recognition of the Oder-Neisse frontier (and they could always depreciate it as a mere sleight of hand), and even his advocacy of more social contacts with East Germany,[43] as long as his general posture toward the Soviet Union and the communist regimes in East Europe seemed one of uncompromising firmness. That stood in desirable contrast with the apparent willingness of the United States to pursue a detente with the Soviet Union, even though the United States had been more restrained than De Gaulle on the subject of the Oder-Neisse frontier. But a France "soft" both in its over-all Eastern policy and on the subject of the Oder-Neisse boundary was hardly preferable to a United States "soft" on the former but reassuring on the latter. Finally, even the fleeting prospect of a Franco-Soviet "Rapallo" was sufficient to give the Germans pause and to make them wonder whether divorce from America was really necessary to consummate the otherwise convenient and desirable Paris-Bonn relationship.

Other West Europeans did not relish the prospect of a Franco-German concert leading West Europe, excluding America, and by itself attempting to regulate with Russia the difficult legacies of World War II. They could take little comfort in the thought that the excluded America would patiently protect Europe from a powerful Soviet Union, while having no voice in the formulation of West European policies —be they passive or aggressive—toward Russia. There was little reason to believe that Washington would give Paris and Bonn a blank check for writing American foreign policy. Most West Europeans welcomed the new cordiality between France and Germany as an essential point of departure for burying the ancient antagonisms that led to the destruction of Europe. They did not welcome, however, a new condominium, and their opposition to it not only bore ill for De Gaulle's vision of a stable Europe but assured the very condition of European fragmentation that all but the Soviets wished to avoid.[44]

Thus although De Gaulle had a vision, he still did not have a policy. His insistence on a Europe detached from America disunited the West without causing any substantial change in the East. Indeed, his attitude could have the effect of driving America out of West Europe (leaving perhaps West Germany as America's last ally) without driving Russia out of East Europe. Precisely for that reason the communist leaders, including the Soviet, encouraged Paris in its pursuit of a "European Europe" even though the concept of a Europe to the Urals was repugnant to them.*

Isolated from America and Germany, France could obstruct, not construct. To heal the European partition Western policy had to satisfy three requirements: the West had to remain sufficiently strong to deter or repel any renewed Soviet pressure; the West had to dispose of enough economic resources to attract the East; the West could not be dominated by Germany, which the East still fears. Committed to the eventual exclusion of America from Europe, De Gaulle could not meet the first two requirements and to many East Euro-

---

* For example, the Hungarian Foreign Minister, who represents a government that still speaks for Moscow, specifically indicated an interest in a "European Europe" on his arrival in Paris in January 1965 at the invitation of the French Government. The Bulgarian, East German, and Soviet press have also pointedly praised the concept of a "European Europe."

peans Europe detached from America seemed more likely to
be led by Germany than by France. Accordingly, France
could not generate a positive and effective policy for East
Europe and Russia, one that could command not only the
visionary enthusiasm of the West and East Europeans, which
in many respects it did, but also their actual energies, which
in most respects it could not. Five years after De Gaulle
launched his vision of Europe to the Urals, its links to practical politics still remained to be shaped. There seemed little
likelihood that this could be done without the participation
of the United States.

The United States—the Problem of Means and Ends

For most of the postwar period the United States has had
no real policy for East Europe. The policy of containment had
not been designed to repair the European division. It was a
militarily defensive reaction against the Soviet threat, meant
to defend the West and eventually to prompt evolutionary
changes in the communist world. Formulated at a time of an
acute Soviet threat to West Europe, it was concerned neither
with exploiting Soviet weakness in East Europe nor with assuaging Soviet fears. Most problems were viewed through the
prism of the balance of military power in Europe, and the
tendency to exaggerate the actual military dimension of
the Soviet threat* had the effect of generating a predominant
preoccupation with Western military preparedness, including
the rearmament of Germany. It resulted in what Jacques Frey-

* "Time and again the United States has credited the Soviet armed forces with
greater strength or combat readiness then has turned out to be warranted," writes
A. Dallin, the principal author of *The Soviet Union and Arms Control,* a special
report prepared for the U.S. Arms Control and Disarmament Agency in 1963–64,
mimeographed, p. 165. In June 1950 a memorandum prepared by a group of
German generals credited the Soviet Army with no less than 265 divisions armed
with "'first-class weapons," and these estimates were widely shared in the United
States. (*United Nations World,* June 1950, as cited by H. B. Price, *The Marshall
Plan and its Meaning,* Ithaca, N.Y., 1955, p. 358.) Finally, in 1963 the widely
accepted figure of approximately 170 Soviet divisions was reduced by official estimates to about 70. (R. T. Rockingham Gill, "The New East-West Military Balance," *East Europe,* April 1964).

mond aptly described as "the militarization of Western thought."

It is a matter of guesswork whether it might have been possible to achieve German reunification, at the cost of some restrictions on German rearmament, immediately after Stalin's death, when the Soviet leadership is said to have been badly split over the future of East Germany. In any case, no serious consideration was given to this alternative at that time.

Eisenhower's policy of liberation ostensibly was meant to correct that deficiency: using containment as a foundation for initiatives designed to weaken the Soviet hold over East Europe, its long-range goal was said to be the "liberation" of the area. It was strongly implied at the time that the United States would exploit any opportunity that might develop in the East and would deter Soviet counteractions, especially with regard to insurrections. Tied to the simultaneous and accelerated West German rearmament, this policy simply disregarded the factors that perpetuated the European division. For its success it depended entirely on the Western and particularly the American willingness to use its military superiority to bring about, through pressure or threat, the desired changes.

Events in East Europe, such as the East German uprising of 1953 or the Hungarian revolution of 1956, revealed the basic hollowness of the policy, and its essentially sloganeering character. Since neither the force nor the will to implement it were available, the proclaimed policy became merely another name for the initial policy of containment.[45]

The shaping of American involvement in East Europe began only around 1957. The success of Gomulka in gaining and holding power in Poland encouraged the United States in the belief that cautious economic aid and the fostering of cultural contacts would assist Poland in maintaining its autonomy and that eventually this would have a contagious effect on the other East European states. In this it differed from the earlier policy of support for Yugoslavia, which actually had asserted its independence of the Soviet bloc. Undertaken as an isolated act and not yet a matter of broad policy, American aid to Poland became available only after the most critical phase in Polish-Soviet relations had passed. Nonetheless, it was doubtless important in enabling the Poles to maintain their new and relaxed agricultural policy and encouraged them to protect their autonomy, even if it did not prevent subsequently the closer identification in foreign policy between Moscow and Warsaw and the curtailment in domestic freedoms. Thus gradually and quite pragmatically a novel approach toward East Europe began to develop, in some ways drawing lessons from the experience gained in aiding Yugoslavia after the Stalin-Tito break, but applying it to a country that remained solidly tied to the Soviet bloc.

The basic assumption of the new approach was that mere verbal hostility would not overthrow the communist regimes and that events in East Germany and Hungary had demonstrated that the West did not have the will to use force. Instead of waiting for the communist regimes to collapse, the United States would henceforth bank on promoting evolutionary changes within them and within the bloc as a whole. In the pursuit of this policy the United States took the initiative, rather ahead of the West European nations, in developing cultural contacts with the Soviet Union and with some of the East European nations. These contacts, according to an official report,[46] were most extensive with Poland, followed by the Soviet Union, the other East European states lagging considerably behind. (Exchanges with Czechoslovakia, Bulgaria, Hungary, and Rumania were negligible and there were none with East Germany or Albania.) While in the Polish and Soviet case the level of American cultural and educational contacts did not come close to those maintained by America with West Europe, U.S. cultural relations with Poland were at least comparable to, and, in the Soviet case, ahead of similar West European efforts.*

* Generous grants from American foundations made their further expansion possible. For example, in August 1964, the Ford Foundation granted $2.3 million for

After failure to respond quickly to the October 1956 developments in Poland (in spite of President Eisenhower's almost immediate promise of economic assistance), the United States did eventually grant Poland, between 1957 and 1963, a total of almost $900 million, and for a time both Poland and Yugoslavia were granted "most favored nation" status by the United States.[47] The Polish case provided a precedent for the rapidly concluded American-Rumanian agreement of mid-1964, which indicated the quickening of American reflexes to changes in the communist camp.

The important effect of economic aid was to give the ruling elites more external options, once they had asserted (even if only partially) their autonomy of Moscow's control or once they had set out on the course of internal liberalization. Nowhere did American economic aid effect internal liberalization; in Hungary liberalization took place without American aid, in Poland and in Yugoslavia retrogressive measures were subsequently adopted while the aid was coming in.* But the availability of the aid reduced the Soviet capacity to use its economic power for blackmail purposes, and improved the East European bargaining position with Moscow,

---

the expansion of scholar-exchange programs with the communist states. The total number of Americans involved in exchanges with the Soviet Union during the six-year period since 1958 was approximately 5,500; during the same period, approximately 4,600 Soviet citizens were involved. However, as noted earlier in regard to West European experience (see Chapter Two), communist fears, especially of the written word, and their desire to control the awards of Western fellowships to their scholars, meant that in all cases the cultural-scientific relations were subject to formal arrangements, either between the governments concerned, or, as in the American-Polish case, between the relevant institutions and organizations. This often resulted in tensions and conflicts, especially between the American interest in the broader social and cultural ramifications of the exchanges and the communist emphasis on their more technologically utilitarian aspects. Thus the Soviet Union has been unwilling to allow the open sale even of American technical books in the USSR, in spite of provisions for that in the cultural agreements, has not implemented the 1958 Radio-Television exchanges agreement, and has been reluctant in permitting U.S. exhibitions to be held in the Soviet Union.

* However, the desire on the part of some regimes for an improvement in relations with the United States did lead to some lessening in domestic coercion. The amnesties in Hungary and Rumania were clearly related to the problem of relations with the United States.

forcing Moscow to increase its own economic aid to East Europe. The primary beneficiary of the aid accordingly was nationalism, not internal freedom. But this was a welcome step forward for a region in which for a decade neither nationalism nor democracy had been respected.

Under President Kennedy the policy of more active but peaceful economic and cultural engagement in East Europe became official doctrine.[48] Its implementation, however, was impeded by the Berlin crisis, which tended to reinforce the line of demarcation between East and West. It was only in the atmosphere of the detente after the Cuban missile crisis that conditions for the pursuit of this policy again became ripe.

However, the detente with the Soviet Union simultaneously created difficulties for American relations with West Europe, and consequently also affected negatively the application of the new policy toward East Europe. To many Europeans it seemed that the United States considered the detente as an end in itself. De Gaulle was able to capitalize on the widespread suspicion that Kennedy agreed with Mao Tse-tung that Europe was a secondary theater of confrontation (unlike De Gaulle and Khrushchev who in different ways continued to attach primary importance to Europe) and that the United States would happily settle for the European status quo, including the present division. Many West Europeans construed the conclusion of the Test Ban Agreement between the "Anglo-Saxons" and the Russians (as well as the "hot line" between Washington and Moscow) as part of the American effort to establish a direct bilateral relationship with Russia over the heads of the Europeans, and basically at the cost of the Europeans, particularly of the West Germans and the East Europeans (whose diplomats privately expressed concern).

This continental reaction highlighted a basic problem of our European policy. That policy "needed" Russia either as an adversary or as an object of policy. The Marshall Plan was successful because Russia performed the role of the adversary. The policy of detente implied, however, a Soviet-American partnership based on a mutual interest in the status quo. The moment this impression was created, the dissipation of American leadership began. Washington played into the hands of De Gaulle and gave Adenauer no option but to sympathize with the French attitude. Washington's seeming eagerness for an American-Soviet detente, almost as an end in itself, ignored a very important psychological dimension: the division of Germany was tolerable only so long as it was accompanied by a measure of hostility toward the Soviet partitioner and especially by frequent American rededications to the elimination of the partition; based on apparent United States cordiality for the occupier the division became the source of frustration and embitterment.

Yet many critics of the detente ignored the benefits which could be derived from it by the West, *provided* the West took advantage of the new opportunities. Only in a relaxed international atmosphere could the hidden tensions and contradictions that plague the East surface and become politically important. The communist regimes, more than the pluralistic West, require hostility and tension to maintain their unity. It is impossible to think of the Hungarian revolution or the Polish October without the "spirit of Geneva" which created a climate of relaxation; it is likewise impossible to consider the Rumanian self-assertion of 1964 occurring in the context of the war-threatening Berlin crisis. Detente inevitably challenges Soviet control over East Europe. Prolonged stability, with the ideological revisions concerning a "peaceful transition to socialism" (a castrated revolution), tends to demoralize even the communist cadres,[49] and the development of stabler relations inescapably opens the East to Western influences.

This posed a paradox for American policy. Detente was necessary to change gradually the status quo, and the failure of the "liberation" concept left no alternative but that of effecting gradual change. Yet an American-Soviet detente on the basis of the European status quo was inherently unstable—it frustrated some West Europeans and reawakened Soviet expectations. Accordingly, the American-Soviet detente had to be used by America as a *means* of a policy specifically designed to reduce the Soviet interest in perpetuating the division of Europe. Detente had to be the proclaimed point of departure for steps designed eventually to end the European and the German division, a goal to which few Europeans could object.

The speech to the Free University of West Berlin, delivered on June 26, 1963, by President Kennedy, stressing the American commitment to the reunification of Europe, indicated that this line of thought was finally gaining ground in Washington. In early 1964 it was further developed in an address by Secretary of State Rusk (February 25), which stressed the need for the West to treat the communist states in a differentiated manner, and which defined the United States purpose as being "to encourage evolution within the communist world toward national independence, peaceful cooperation, and open societies." *

The Secretary followed this with assurances to the NATO ministerial council in May 1964 that there was no "true detente" between the United States and the Soviet Union, and that there were no secret talks between the Soviet Union and the United States concerning the fate of Europe. Finally, on May 31, 1964, President Johnson, in his speech on "building bridges to the East," linked German reunification with an improvement in relations with East Europe: "It is our belief that wise and skillful development of relationships with the nations of Eastern Europe can speed the day when Germany will be reunited."

While far from assuaging the fears of the West German critics of the American-Soviet detente, the President in effect was articulating a Western policy designed to be the response

* He was echoed a few days later by the Undersecretary of State Averell Harriman (in testimony of March 10, before the Subcommittee on Europe of the House of Representatives), who amplified Rusk's definition of U.S. goals: "We hope to see, and are trying to encourage, a progressive loosening of external authority over Eastern European countries and the continuing reassertion of national autonomy and diversity. We believe such evolution is a slow but sure way toward freedom and national independence. . . . Our policy is to encourage the evolution now in progress by using every kind of peaceful contact available."

to the Soviet policy of fragmentation. These new formulations gave more focus to the various American efforts pursued since 1957.* President Johnson's formulation was especially significant in that it made German unification dependent on changes in Eastern Europe. It marked the final abandonment of the notion that the German problem could be settled outside of, or prior to, an over-all change in the relations between the two halves of Europe.[50] But it also meant that the American policy on the German question had to be reexamined critically, lest it conflict with America's larger Eastern policy. Such a reexamination was long overdue.

On the German issue it seems justified to charge that the United States has led where it should have followed, and followed where it should have led. The United States has supported the West German view on the frontier issue and has maintained that the eastern frontier of a reunited Germany would be settled at a "peace conference." This contradicted directly the basic assumption of the policy of establishing closer relations with East Europe: namely, the expectation that eventually East Europe would evolve its own freedom and the puppet regime in East Germany would become untenable for the Soviet Union. General de Gaulle understood better than Washington that as long as there is the slightest doubt in Poland and Czechoslovakia concerning the long-range German territorial intentions, the vast majority of the

---

* The emerging American policy could be described as favoring a "marginal" approach; many of the other solutions often advocated out of despair or frustration could be described as "systemic." The terms "marginal" and "systemic" are borrowed from Robert A. Levine's *The Arms Debate*, Cambridge, 1963. He used the former to describe gradual pursuit of a long-range goal through marginal steps and the latter as involving a more basic change in the existing system.

Indeed, in the past the proclaimed policy of liberation had been a systemic policy; its implementation would have dramatically transformed the political map of Europe. The Soviet policy of "breakthrough" had been also a systemic policy: the removal of Western forces from West Berlin, the formal recognition of the division of Germany, and the fragmentation of NATO were meant to effect a qualitative change in the balance of power. (Failure to perceive this led some Western observers to be relatively uncritical about the Soviet solutions for Berlin. For example, see F. D. Neal, *War and Peace and Germany*, New York, 1962.) The failure of both sides led them toward marginal policies, even though their goals may have basically remained the same.

Poles and Czechs will favor a policy of close support for the maintenance of the Soviet-sponsored buffer in East Germany.

American support for the formal German position on the frontier issue did not stem, by and large, from any sympathy for the revision of the existing Oder-Neisse boundary. Accordingly, Washington could assure the Poles privately that the West neither expected nor favored any changes in the existing frontiers. But in the absence of public American commitments, the Polish government could continue to represent the Polish-Soviet alliance as the only guarantee for the existing frontier. It could publicly charge the United States with rearming the one European country with major territorial claims on Poland. It could accuse (and even discredit) Radio Free Europe, which has been the major source of noncommunist information in Poland, of being silent on the subject of the Oder-Neisse line on orders issued by the State Department in deference to West Germany. All of that played into Warsaw's hands, and defeated the broader aims of American policy.

American *immobilisme* on this subject, apart from the inherent difficulty of changing a posture once adopted (the initial formulation of the American wait-and-see position on the Polish-German frontier was made at the very beginning of the cold war), was largely due to the fear that anything less would be considered by the allied Germans as a betrayal of their interests on behalf of an adversary nation. Not being able to effect German reunification, so went the argument, the least the United States could do was not to give up existing German claims. Anything less would set the stage for a new German-Soviet Rapallo. The Russians would reward the Germans with Polish territory and the Germans would leave NATO and destroy Western unity. America therefore could not move ahead of West Germany on the frontier issue but must await a change in the German position.* Alternatively,

* The Rapallo argument was based on a misplaced historical analogy. In 1922 Germany and the new Soviet Russia were both weak international outcasts. The Rapallo agreement between them was made from a position of equality. In 1939, Nazi Germany and Stalinist Russia were both aggressive and relatively secure

it was sometimes argued that a change in the American pos-
ture would play into the hands of the French; however, the
French position was already in favor of recognition of the
Oder-Neisse frontier.

However, as long as Washington seemed to be supporting
the formal German position on the legality of the 1937 frontiers, it was more difficult, given the context of competitive
democratic politics, for a German politician or party to seem
more yielding on an issue involving national emotions than is
the case with a foreign government, i.e., the United States.
Even though most Germans realize that they stand alone on
the question of the Oder-Neisse line, the mere fact of formal
American support for the legal position that the frontier is
still to be "settled" undercut those German leaders who did
realize that the way to reunification includes also the necessity
of a German-Polish reconciliation. It also reduced the political
significance of the American effort to "build bridges" to East
Europe.

While America followed instead of taking the lead on
the issue of the Oder-Neisse frontier, on occasions it tended
to lead rather than follow on the issue that to Germany was of
much more immediate interest: East Germany. From the
standpoint of the German-American alliance and of a common
Western policy toward the East, it is essential that the United
States should not recognize the division of Germany as permanent. Any policies or statements even *implicitly* contributing to
the perpetuation of that division, would serve to fragment the
Western alliance and would play into Soviet hands. The issue
of East Germany was one in which it behooves America to be
guided by German estimates and desires, and, if anything,

nations; the agreement was again made on a basis of rough equality. In 1965, or
at any foreseeable future date, an agreement between the western part of trun-
cated Germany and the Soviet Union, the former relatively weak, the latter the
second military power in the world, would not be an act of German diplomacy
but an act of national suicide. It would mean that the West Germans were plac-
ing themselves at the mercy of Russia and depriving themselves of American
protection for the sake of territorial awards from a country that would subsequently also have the power to deny them.

even to appear less conciliatory toward Pankow than Bonn, so that Washington can never be accused by the Germans of accepting the German partition.

Yet at times the United States seemed to be moving considerably ahead of West Germany and disregarding German feelings on this vitally alive *German* issue, while timidly toeing the West German line with regard to the boundary issue involving not only Germany *and* East Europe but also America and East Europe. During the initial phases of the detente, there was widespread suspicion in Germany that the United States might "settle" for the division of Germany in return for peace around Berlin.[51] This inclination had been nurtured by certain American proposals made during the more acute stages of the Berlin crisis, particularly the so-called "international access authority" concept. In April 1962 the American government proposed that the responsibility for access to West Berlin be assumed by an international body, composed of five Western powers (U.S., U.K., France, Federal German Republic, and West Berlin), five communist states (USSR, Poland, Czechoslovakia, East Germany, and East Berlin) and three neutral states (Austria, Sweden, and Switzerland). In addition, according to one source, the State Department proposed an exchange of non-aggression declarations betwween NATO and the members of the Warsaw Treaty and requested West German approval for the scheme on a 24-hour notice.[52] Within days the East Germans hailed the proposal,[53] while West German chagrin was evident to all.[54]

The American proposal was nothing short of a unilateral American concession on an issue of vital and direct national importance to Germany. First of all, since the Eastern and the Western powers on the proposed body would be equally matched, responsibility for access would have been shifted to three small and neutral powers, not a single one of them with a direct stake or vested interest in West Berlin. Secondly, the proposal implied parity between East and West Germany since both were to be on the same footing in the proposed authority. Thus a major step enhancing the international status of East Germany would have been taken. Although subsequently the proposal was quietly dropped (in large measure due to violent West German opposition), its total effect was to weaken German confidence in American leadership and in the viability of the German-American alliance. It generated some of the intense enthusiasm that for a time some Germans displayed in favor of a closer association with DeGaulle. It also strengthened the latent feeling that only direct negotiations between Bonn and Moscow could resolve the German problem.

More recently, in 1964, the impression became widespread in Germany that the United States was encouraging the West Germans to establish closer ties with the East Germans, along the lines urged by Brandt. For instance, this feeling was reinforced by the grant of U.S. export licenses for the sale of a synthetic fiber plant to East Germany by two American companies. Bonn had not been consulted, although this sale equalled the total American exports to East Germany over the last few years. Thus again the American attitude seemed to go beyond what ought to be its limiting consideration: that on the issue of relations with East Germany, the United States must first respect West German feelings, lest a more nationalistic German leadership be able to accuse the United States at some future point of having contributed to the international acceptance of the German partition.

Leaving aside the obviously complex and difficult German problem (concerning which more will be said in the conclusion), the initial implementation of the new American policy of differentiated penetration of East Europe posed another danger: that eventually the means of policy might become its end. The policy of "building bridges" involved necessarily a series of sporadic and pragmatic efforts to improve relations with the ruling communist governments, unlike the policy of containment, which ignored both the East European peoples and their governments, and the policy of liberation, which addressed itself primarily to the peoples. Without substantial improvement in relations with the ruling governments, the new policy would remain a purely declarative one. It was probably because of this that the U.S. dispensed with the earlier, much more precise formulation of American goals, particularly the long-standing insistence on the holding of free elections as provided by the Yalta agreements, articulated on March 16, 1950, by the then Secretary of State Dean Acheson.* Continued insistence on the holding of free elections could jeopardize the improvement in official relations. Dropping this insistence, however, meant that it was no longer clear whether the American goal for East Europe was, for example, the status of Finland or that of Rumania.

Furthermore, on the operational level there was an inescapable bureaucratic inclination to judge the success of the policy by the degree of cordiality generated within East European official circles for American officials. This posed the danger that the policy would become one of "undifferentiated differentiation"—its success being measured by the willingness of the regimes to have formally good relations with the United States and to accept American aid, neither of which any longer constituted defiance of the Soviet Union, without substantive changes either in their domestic or external policies. The inclination of De Gaulle to court the Eastern states, without much regard either to their internal or external politics, was also contributing to an undifferentiated Western competition in courting the East, at the cost of political objectives. The concentration on the goodwill of the governments tended to leave the people out of the equation, with the result that the governments concerned might eventually feel less inhibited in

---

* "What concerns us is that [these governments] should be truly independent national regimes, with a will of their own and with a decent foundation in popular feeling. . . . Nothing would so alter the international climate as the holding of elections in the satellite states *in which the true will of the people could be expressed*." Address delivered at the University of California, Berkeley; Department of State *Bulletin,* March 27, 1950, pp. 473–478. *American Foreign Policy,* Vol. II, p. 1932 (italics added).

impeding domestic democratization and in asserting their control.*

The implementation of the new American policy was further complicated by the widespread inclination of the American press to exaggerate and sensationalize the newly developing ties between the United States and the East European states. Thus the American-Rumanian agreement was interpreted even by the leading U.S. newspapers almost as an act of Rumanian defection to the West and as a great triumph for American diplomacy. Perhaps this had been necessary to overcome Congressional opposition,† but it embarrassed the Rumanians, and it may have even inhibited the other East European states from emulating the Rumanian example. In contrast, French spokesmen and the French press handled the subsequent Rumanian-French agreement with far greater tact and diplomacy. Both went out of their way to emphasize that the agreement was a modest one (in fact it was not more so than the American-Rumanian one) and that it did not in any way undermine the basic associations of the respective countries with the two European systems of alliance. The Rumanian leaders returned home from Paris impressed with the restraint and delicatesse of the French negotiators and less fearful of possible repercussions in Moscow.‡

Communist reactions to the new American policy high-

* For example, on April 4, 1964, a Washington spokesman justified the extension of American aid to Poland on the grounds that "there has been a far greater degree of freedom of speech in Poland since 1956, and the intellectual activity in that country is stimulating and lively." Yet at that very time within Poland the intellectual community, sparked by a letter from 34 of its leaders submitted to the Prime Minister in late March and pleading for more liberal cultural policy, was protesting measures designed to subject it to stricter controls. Similarly in Bulgaria, anti-American demonstrations, organized by the government in connection with an espionage show trial, were followed by cordial invitations to high Bulgarian officials to visit Washington.

† Persisting Congressional suspicion of any rapprochement with the communist states resulted in the adoption in 1964 of amendments to Public Law 480, prohibiting the sale of surplus American farm products to Poland for Polish currency, thereby reducing the Administration's freedom of maneuver.

‡ The Soviet press did print the French-Rumanian communique, whereas it did not the American-Rumanian one.

lighted these problems. First of all, there was evidence of some East European apprehension lest Soviet suspicions be aroused by a too conspicuous cordiality toward the United States, in view of the American penchant for extreme interpretations. Secondly, and more important, some communist commentators were openly concerned that the new American policy might prove efficacious in promoting Western penetration of the communist world, intensifying the differences among its members, and softening the regimes' ability to resist.* However, in spite of these fears, the communist leaders were inclined to respond affirmatively to the new American approach. Their hope was that gradually they might succeed in emasculating it of its political content. Increasingly reassured that the West cannot contest their power, they could more easily afford some domestic concessions in return for United States acceptance and economic aid, while concentrating their propaganda on the theme of the German danger.

The new American policy, regardless of its good beginnings and its basically right direction, still suffered from vagueness concerning the American goals in East Europe and from contradictions with respect to the German question. President Johnson's formulation had neither the visionary quality of De Gaulle's "Europe to the Urals" nor the specificity of Acheson's earlier definition of goals. The fact that the frequency of public expressions of the American interest in East Europe increased in direct proportion to the proximity of American Presidential elections hardly enhanced the credibility of the occasional American commitments.

Just what sort of an Eastern Europe were we seeking and were we justified in realistically expecting? What did we hope to accomplish by encouraging East European nationalisms? The communist willingness to develop economic and cultural

* For example, the editor of the authoritative Warsaw weekly, *Polityka*, M. Rakowski, on May 9, 1964, in a lengthy analysis of the new policy "Doctrines Change—The Purpose Remains," warned that it is aimed at "the weakening of the position, of the offensive capacity, and at the dulling of the dynamism" of world communism. For some similar Hungarian reactions, see Nemes, *op. cit.*

contacts emphasized the more complex nature of the present game: both sides were prepared to play it according to the same rules but with each interpreting his own score. Without clearer and more reasoned answers, there was the real danger that the American effort could become dissipated in a euphoria of politically meaningless goodwill. Greater discrimination in techniques and more selective criteria for applying flexibly a policy of cordiality and, whenever necessary, also its opposite, were required to give the new approach a sharper political edge. Otherwise, it could become a disguised way of settling for the status quo.

Last but not least, American policy for the East has to be designed with one ear cocked for West European reactions. Unless America takes the lead in formulating a policy designed to captivate the imaginations of all Europeans and to involve them in the common venture of building Europe, there are mounting prospects that a "European Europe" of smaller nationalist states will by default seek its own accommodation with Russia, with all the dangers that this would pose for America's continued relationship to Europe and for Europe itself.

CHAPTER FOUR

Peaceful Engagement in Europe's Future

The partition of Europe is the outcome of a historical process spanning two world wars. The European restoration accordingly cannot be accomplished by a single political settlement. Neither will it come about by American or Russian disengagement from Europe. America and Russia will not abandon Europe, for neither could be certain that its departure would not mean the extension of the power of the other—no matter what formal guarantees were provided. Moreover, De Gaulle's oratory notwithstanding, Europe in the foreseeable future will not be powerful enough to end its own partition. This partition can only be ended if the American-Soviet confrontation in Europe is gradually transformed into cooperation. That requires both patience and imagination. And it does not exclude an occasional bold initiative, designed to make the gradual process take a qualitative step forward.

De Gaulle once wrote that great leaders are remembered "for the sweep of their endeavors." This is true of great nations as well. Their leadership is measured not only by their power but also by the scope of their goals. Commitment to a grand goal can generate the power of attraction and mobilize adherents. Leadership is a dynamic—not a static—condition. It expands with the tasks undertaken.

Today, America faces a great and growing challenge: to take the initiative toward ending the partition of Europe. In present circumstances, merely to strive to tie West Europe to America in order to defend it from Russia will only awaken

European suspicions of American hegemony, especially as the European fear of Russia wanes and the European sense of dependence on America declines. New security schemes, such as the MLF, even if otherwise desirable, will not solve the problem of the American-European relationship, for the problem is now less one of European security than of the *purpose* of the relationship. There is widespread evidence of growing European feeling that America is becoming irrelevant to the future of a divided, safe, but somehow frustrated Europe. The fact that De Gaulle's appeals for a "European Europe," including a "Europe to the Urals," have been evoking an increasingly sympathetic reaction among a growing number of Europeans and the fact that German politics give every sign of mounting restlessness, are testimony to the proposition that a new era is dawning in Europe, that a new European mood is shaping. This new condition has special implications for America's relationship to Europe.

By taking the initiative in developing policies designed to bring both Russia and East Europe into a closer relationship with the West, and thereby to end the European partition, America would be furthering its own basic interests. First of all, the very fact of such commitment would do much to revive America's waning relevance to Europe. Secondly, it would provide a framework for restoring the East European nations to independence without simultaneously creating new instabilities or stimulating narrow nationalisms. Finally, by laying the foundations for a broader East-West settlement, it would eliminate the persisting European fears of an American-Soviet power duopoly. All that would be consistent with domestic American values and the American quest for world order.

It is sometimes said that a Europe free from America would be in a better position to solve the problem of its partition. Such a Europe would seem less threatening to Russia and East Europe, hence they would be more inclined to accept a closer relationship with it. But this view overlooks the probability that the process of achieving such an "independent" Europe, detached from America, would cause conflicts and instabilities which the Russians already are exploiting. Second, and just as important, such a Europe would probably be dominated by Germany (see Table XVI), and hence would be unlikely to offer an appealing magnet to the East Europeans and to the Russians. Because the United States has no claims beyond the Elbe, its continued association with Europe offers the best guarantee to the Russians and the East Europeans that the West poses no direct political threat to them.

As far as the West Europeans are concerned, our pursuit of the goal of peaceful reunification of Europe is more likely to command European support than either our past calls for "liberation" or our present attempts to develop a more equitable control of nuclear weapons, not to mention our efforts to involve Europe in the rather remote problems of Asian or African development. Such a broader design could displace the Gaullist appeal, or even preempt eventual Gaullist approaches to Russia. Moreover it would mitigate the danger that the disintegration of Western unity would leave the American-German alliance as the sole bond between America and Europe.

A bilateral German-American relationship could only be defensive; it would have no appeal in East Europe and no constructive Eastern policy could be based on it alone. Such a relationship could perhaps provide a shield for West Europe, but its effectiveness in this respect would paradoxically contribute to further divisions in the West. European dissensions would flourish in the protected haven provided by American-German power. There would be little room for America in such a Europe, and eventually even the German-American ties might crumble as their inability to assure German reunification became more evident.

Three cardinal assumptions should guide American policy in the pursuit of the goal of European restoration:

First, *Western military strength must be maintained and*

Western interests vigorously protected. This point may be self-evident. But military strength is a prerequisite as much for policies of increasing cooperation and eventual conciliation, as for policies of pressure and hostility. Precisely because both the objectives and the means of the policy advocated here are peaceful, it is important that there be no uncertainty on the other side as to the West's determination to protect its interests. If the status quo is to be the starting point for an eventual reconciliation, it follows that the West must remain vigilant in protecting it.

The Soviets have provided much evidence over the last two decades that they consider Berlin an exposed Western outpost, vulnerable to pressure. Occasional acts of Soviet pressure may, therefore, be expected. They ought to be resisted, for even a few hours' interruption of access to Berlin undermines the Western position. The final release of a Western convoy after a 50-hour delay represents not a Western victory, but a proof of the Soviet capacity to interrupt access. Responses more vigorous than those heretofore are needed in the future. Since the United States has indicated that it will not invade Cuba, Cuba could perhaps serve as a useful hostage for Berlin. Soviet-engineered delays in our right of access to Berlin should perhaps be immediately reciprocated by similar harassment of Soviet shipping on the international waters around Cuba. Exactly because that action would be arbitrary, it would drive home to the Soviet leadership the lesson that the West will tolerate no impairment of its present position.

The fundamental point is that no Western policy of conciliation is possible in a context which allows the other side opportunities for effective military blackmail. The historical significance of the Cuban confrontation was that it deflated the confidence of Soviet leaders in their ability to extort concessions from the West by military threats. We must never allow them to think they can.

Second, *any basic change in the East-West European relationship will have to involve East Europe jointly with Russia.*

A policy based on the assumption that individual East European states can be encouraged to defect to the West is not likely to succeed because in the final analysis the ruling communist elites have no interest in becoming absorbed by the West, even though pushed in that direction by economic and popular pressures. The Soviet Union is likely to exert every effort to prevent open defections either from CEMA or from the Warsaw Treaty Organization. Moreover, the experience of Yugoslavia and Poland suggests that ruling communist elites gravitate back toward a closer relationship with Moscow once the more objectionable aspects of their relationship with the Soviet Union have been eliminated. Their defections were thus limited and revocable.

Indeed, defections of the East European countries individually, even if possible, might not be in the interest of peace. The United States and the Soviet Union will remain for a long time to come the two leading competitors for global power. Hence dramatic change either way—the defection of the East European states to the West or the fragmentation of West Europe and the expulsion of America—would directly threaten the present balance of power and set in motion dangerous reactions and counter-reactions. In addition, individual defections, especially if the result of encouragement from the West, would reduce the moderating influence of East Europe on Russia, and thus decelerate the ultimately crucial process of Russian evolution.

The more desirable sequence of change would begin with the internal liberalization of the East European societies and lead toward their gradual evolution into a Greater Europe jointly with the Soviet Union. This obviously does not mean a synchronized evolution. East Europe, given its historical links with the West and in some cases more advanced internal conditions prior to communist take-over, is likely to evolve more rapidly than Russia. This is especially true of Czechoslovakia, and to a lesser extent of Hungary and Poland. While it would be unrealistic to expect these East European countries soon to become democratic societies, or to leave the communist orbit, their more rapid evolution may accelerate a similar evolution in the Soviet Union, precisely because they remain linked to it. In its turn, change in the Soviet Union may stimulate further changes in those East European states which, for historical reasons, lag behind Russia. Thus East Europe, while not breaking away from the Soviet Union, may pull the Soviet Union forward by moving ahead of it, thereby cumulatively preparing the ground for a better East-West relationship.

Not that we should actively discourage the occasional acts of nationalist self-assertion, as for instance in the case of Rumania. Bucharest's nationalist self-assertion automatically reduced the restrictive influence of the Soviet Union on East Europe. To the extent that Moscow was compelled to reconsider its own heavy-handed economic nationalism in dealings with the East European states, the development was all to the good. Its importance, however, should not be overrated. It is doubtful that a healthy Europe can be built by promoting anti-Soviet nationalist dictatorships. They could bring in their wake all the traditional territorial and ethnic conflicts, providing temptations for the Soviet Union and the United States again to become involved. It would be short-sighted for the West to ride the tiger of nationalism in the hope that it will threaten only the Soviet dominated world; the tiger could endanger all of Europe.

Third, *the end of the division of Germany will come only as a consequence of a gradual but qualitative change in the relationship between both Russia and East Europe and the West.* In all likelihood, German reunification will be the last and not the first act in the evolutionary unification of the European continent. It will come about through a process of change, and it is not likely to be the outcome of some far-reaching diplomatic settlement around a green table. At long last, German, French, and American policies have come to recognize this reality. But this recognition carries with it additional implications for our perspective on such problems as the Berlin wall and the issue of the Eastern frontier.

Painful as it may be to acknowledge, the wall has increased the long-range prospects for German reunification. As long as East Germany was being drained by massive defections of its population, the situation became increasingly unstable and the front line confrontation on the German demarcation line was intensified. Since the Soviet Union was far from ready to resign itself to the dismantling of the East German regime, the tension forced a further assertion of the Soviet presence in East Germany and reinforced Soviet domination throughout the adjacent regions. Moreover, the events of 1953 and 1956 show the improbability of Western intervention in support of a major rebellion in East Germany. Accordingly, the tensions and the massive flights increased the hostility between the East and the West without in any way increasing the prospects that the dividing line could be erased.

The Berlin wall, however, provides the West with a striking symbol of the basic artificiality of the East German regime without the dangers inherent in the daily exposure and exacerbation of that artificiality. More important, the relative quiet on the German front line permits Western maneuvers in East Europe designed to stimulate evolutionary changes. The East Europeans were more responsive because of the seeming security provided by the buffer East German state. The cumulative effect of the wall is thus clearly in the West's, including Germany's, long-range interest, despite the anguish and demoralization it causes.

Moreover, the shifting of the central focus of the European problem from Germany to East Europe has created more favorable conditions for a more genuine enlistment of British and French support for the cause of European reunification. Although paying lip service to the proposition that Germany should be reunified, neither could look forward with equanimity to the prospect of a reunified, 70-million-strong, Germany, by far the strongest European power [see Table XVI]. But though a mere shift of the European partition from the Elbe to the Oder River, with East Europe in the Russian sphere and West Europe dominated by Germany, is not ap-

pealing to non-German Western Europeans, a broader solution involving East Europe and Russia could mobilize the
support even of those who fear Germany, and make their commitment to German reunification more than a hollow ritual.
This broader solution, however, requires a normalization of
Germany's relationship with East Europe, particularly on the
critical issue of Germany's eastern frontier.

Five Policy Goals

Western policies in Europe thus should be based on three
main premises: the maintenance of Western military power,
the joint involvement of Eastern Europe and Russia in any
ultimate solution, and the interdependence of German reunification with evolutionary change in the East. These premises
are related and the policy goals they imply should be pursued
simultaneously. The West cannot solve the German problem
without developing policies which transcend it and encompass
the whole range of problems associated with the division of
Europe. Western policy should, then, have five goals:

1. *To convince the East Europeans, particularly the
Czechs and the Poles, that the existence of East Germany
limits their freedom without enhancing their security.* Otherwise, the Czechs and the Poles will continue to support the
Soviet presence in East Germany as a convenient and reassuring buffer against the West. To undermine the East European
stake in East Germany, the West will have to differentiate
sharply between its attitude toward East Germany and toward
the rest of East Europe. For East Germany, the policy must
be one of isolation; for East Europe, one of peaceful engagement—economic, cultural, and eventually political. Only then
will East Germany become a political anachronism on the
map of Europe, a source of continuing embarrassment to
Moscow, and no longer a source of security to the East
Europeans.

The efforts so far undertaken by the West German government to establish closer relations with the East European states have already contributed greatly to isolating the East German regime. To further this process, the West German government should be encouraged to find some way to free itself from the self-imposed limits on relations with the East European states inherent in the Hallstein doctrine. Perhaps excluding from the application of the doctrine those states which are members of the Warsaw Treaty Organization or possibly those that border on Germany could provide a loophole, without encouraging other states to recognize East Germany. In any case, it is only through better relations with West Germany that the East Europeans can eventually become convinced that the reunification of Germany opens to them the doors to the West that are now shut by Soviet occupation forces in East Germany.

Only communist fanatics attach any ideological importance to the continued existence of communist East Germany. For other East Europeans, East Germany is valuable primarily in terms of their largely defensive national interests, but with the progressive evolution of the East European states, skillfully abetted by a conciliatory West, East Germany eventually may lose even its appeal as a buffer, and begin to resemble a Soviet Mozambique—a source of irritation to the East Europeans and of embarrassment to Moscow. Only then will the Kremlin consider the possibility of liquidating the East German regime, and it is only the Kremlin, not the German communists, which *can* consider its liquidation. Creation of conditions for this should be the goal of American and German policy—not merely the transformation of the East German regime into a more moderate communist regime, hence perhaps more acceptable to its own people and to the West.

The ostracism of East Germany can be furthered by treating the East European states as if in fact they were fully independent states, unlike East Germany doomed to remain a mere Soviet puppet. The East European states can gradually evolve because they are national states. Their nationalism works in the direction of maximizing their freedom from *the* one state that now stands in the way of independence—the Soviet Union. Therefore, the United States and the West ought to respond seriously to any East European foreign policy proposals, and even encourage the East Europeans to make more.* Our response to such proposals need not be affirmative, but greater efforts should be made to engage the individual East European states in prolonged discussions and negotiations. These breed national pride, expose East European leaders to Western arguments in relative privacy and free from Soviet supervision, and stimulate an awareness of their own national interest. It is not in the interest of the West to dismiss (as has often been done) the East Europeans as proxies for the Soviet Union, even when they are acting as such.

2. *To promote a German-Polish reconciliation,* somewhat on the model of the Franco-German reconciliation of the fifties. Such a reconciliation should be a proclaimed goal of the United States, the closest ally of Germany and the home of many millions of Americans of both German and Polish ancestry. Just as peace and stability in Western Europe could not have been achieved unless the old Franco-German quarrel was ended, so a German-Polish reconciliation is the sine qua non of peace and stability in the East. The moral prestige of the United States would be enhanced by proclaiming such a reconciliation a principal American objective, in contrast to the policy of the Soviet Union and the communists, who find it convenient to keep the bitter Polish-German hatred alive.

The pursuit of this goal inevitably raises the difficult and sensitive issue of the Oder-Neisse frontier. Perhaps some day frontiers will cease to be important in Europe, but that day will only come after they become accepted and secure. A sense

---

* That this is becoming a more sensitive issue among the East Europeans was suggested to the author by the reaction of a very high East European official when he was asked why his country, unlike communist Poland, did not take any foreign policy initiatives. After an embarrassed silence, he agreed that perhaps his country had been remiss on the international scene and hoped that perhaps in the near future it would become more active in taking international initiatives.

of insecurity about frontier issues keeps alive national hatreds and fears. At the present time, since anti-Germanism is the principal asset of a weak and unpopular Polish regime, it may not be in the interest of the Polish government to reach any substantial agreement with Germany, including on the frontier issue. Indeed, the ideal situation for that government would be to obtain Western economic aid while *not* obtaining but persistently demanding the recognition of the Oder-Neisse frontier. Moreover, it is certainly in the Soviet interest to keep the issue alive. Accordingly, Western moves will have to be designed to dispel the widespread Polish popular fears of the Germans, even in the absence of a formal German-Polish agreement.

In seeking this goal, the United States will have to be careful not to rupture the American-German relationship, on which both the unity of the West and German democracy so much depend. A German feeling that America has betrayed them will certainly not serve the cause of German-Polish reconciliation. The Poles ought to realize this, just as the Germans should see that overcoming the Polish fear of Germany would deprive Moscow of a major asset and would be a major step toward German reunification. Although the Germans are becoming increasingly aware that it is politically self-defeating to demand German reunification without defining precisely the location of Germany's eastern frontiers, a precipitate American recognition of the present frontier would nevertheless provoke bitter resentment in Germany. The United States should proceed by stages, designed to convince the Poles that no one in the West either expects or favors a change in the present frontiers.

A first step which could be taken soon would be to open American consulates either in Szczecin or Wroclaw.[1] This move would be useful both politically and symbolically. Next a NATO pledge to oppose the use of force to change existing European frontiers would help to create the preconditions of a German-Polish reconciliation, since it would lend greater weight to the unilateral German declaration to the same effect made in 1954. The West German government could hardly object to NATO making the same declaration it had made itself. A multilateral Western pledge would be more convincing to the Poles than a pledge by Germany alone, given Germany's possible interest in changing the frontier.

A similar declaration by the President of the United States at some appropriately symbolic occasion (but not during the American electoral season), with specific reference to the desirability of ending the Polish-German feud, would also serve to put to rest an issue which simply keeps alive old hostilities, primarily to the advantage of the Soviet Union. Such a statement could perhaps even be modeled on the several French statements on the frontier issue, made without harm to the Franco-German relationship. An American endorsement would have special significance to the Poles, given the popularity and prestige of America in Poland. Finally, the Western powers could pledge in advance their intention to recognize formally the present frontiers at the moment that Germany is reunified, thereby stimulating a Polish national interest in that reunification, even if the Polish communist government should initially oppose it.

From the standpoint of advancing German reunification, such assurances to Poland would be more productive if made at a time when the Poles are still insecure about the frontier issue. Eventually, their sense of insecurity may fade; the Poles may come to care less for Western guarantees and may derive greater security from the existence of the two German states. German policy should strive to prevent the development of a lasting Polish vested interest in the partition of Germany; it should strive to rekindle instead the bonds of sympathy and cooperation that at various times in history did link these two neighboring states. Only then will a foundation have been laid for an eventual settlement. Without this foundation, the Poles can hardly be expected to see any interest in a settlement of the German issue.

Within West Germany, a nonpartisan political approach may well be required, since it has been said that neither of the two major parties could afford to give the other any opportunity of charging that vital German interests have been sacrificed. A nonpartisan stand, which explicitly links the solemn renunciation of claims to territories lost in the aftermath of World War II to German reunification, and which is presented to the German people as a historical contribution to the reconciliation of the German and Polish peoples, could overcome much of the inevitable resistance from the more nationalistic elements.* Fortunately, the cause of German-Polish reconciliation is growing increasingly popular among German youth. The prior adoption of that stand by the Western allies would reduce the risk of charges in Germany that German politicians are precipitately "betraying" German interests.

In addition, the United States could promote specific undertakings, designed to forge bonds of mutual understanding between the Germans and the Poles, thereby also reemphasizing America's own constructive revelance to Central Europe. To the extent possible, three-way meetings between Americans, Germans, and Poles could be sponsored, in addition to the various bilateral German-Polish activities already in progress. Special emphasis should be put on youth activities; perhaps a fruitful approach would be to encourage joint German-Polish youth activities in the Third World. Collaborative humanitarian efforts could perhaps help to erase the recent memories of conflict and restore the fraternal atmosphere that prevailed among the Germans and the Poles as recently as during "the spring of nations" of 1848.

3. *To lessen the Russian obsession with Germany.* It is probably impossible to eradicate the deeply-held Russian

---

* This would be in keeping with the pledge made to East Europe by Chancellor Erhard on October 15, 1964: "We shall therefore leave nothing untried to demonstrate to these countries again and again that the only hindrance to a mutual reconciliation is the unsolved German question, and that for this reason an early settlement for this issue would be in their own best interests."

fear of the Germans, especially in view of the relatively recent memories of the war. There is also no doubt that the Soviet leaders find it convenient to use Germany as a bogey, and accordingly will take advantage of every opportunity to portray West Germany as militaristic and revanchist. Yet given the slow but still discernible evolutionary trends in Russian society, it is desirable not to stimulate counter pressures or to provoke needless and pointless irritations. The solution for Europe's partition, and for Germany's, will not be found in the context of worsening relations between America and Russia, or of intensified Russian and East European hostility toward Germany.

The kind of policy to be avoided is exemplified by the proposal, occasionally voiced in West Germany, that China be aided as a form of pressure on the Russians. The political argument on behalf of aiding China (leaving aside the purely economic interest of some business circles in obtaining Chinese trade) is based on the thesis that the Soviet Union can eventually be induced to seek an accommodation with the West if it becomes fearful of a new, hostile encirclement. A weak and isolated China, so goes the argument, cannot effectively threaten Russia. Furthermore, a Chinese-West German trade agreement, containing the Berlin clause, will mean the further isolation of East Germany and hence be a step toward eventual reunification. Although in deference to the United States the matter was postponed until after the 1964 American elections, Germans apparently have considered exploring the possibility of concluding with the Chinese first an informal trade agreement, signed perhaps by a consortium of German firms, to be followed later by a more formal arrangement, with the Berlin clause in it, and even including credits.

A more extreme point of view has been taken with regard to China by those Germans, fortunately a minority, who fear a reduction of tensions between Moscow and Washington and who see in China an instrument for upsetting the existing territorial arrangements in Europe.[2] The notion of a "second intermediate zone," directed at both Washington and Moscow, has a special appeal to those who chafe under the apparent restraints of the American-German alliance and who would like to pursue a policy of revision with regard to the territorial status quo.

Yet to follow this course would be to reawaken the relatively dormant European border disputes. This would have a highly divisive effect in the West, where there is a universal lack of support for any change in the existing European frontiers. In Germany itself it would serve to strengthen the extreme right wing and eventually contribute to Germany's isolation in the West. Moreover, it still involves a "political warfare" approach to the problem of German reunification. It could only have the effect of intensifying East Europe's dependence on Russia and of stimulating a new wave of anti-German Russian nationalist sentiments. Such pressure would merely confirm to Moscow what it is prone to assume anyway: that West Germany is unalterably hostile and perhaps even dangerous. It is difficult to see how this would contribute either to the cause of German reunification or to the cause of peace. Indeed, in a self-fulfilling prophecy, it could help to produce an implicit Russian-American alliance dedicated to the preservation of the European status quo, thereby consummating the division of Germany. The road to East Berlin seems hardly shorter by way of Peking.

These considerations suggest why West Germany ought to be very cautious in even exploring trade ties with China. The objective of further isolating East Germany is desirable and perhaps an agreement with China containing the Berlin clause would serve that end.* But it should not be forgotten that China once before, in 1957, signed such an agreement (which later was not renewed), and that this inherently reduces the

* Nervous editorials in *Neues Deutschland* suggest that the East German regime was quite uneasy about this possibility. E.g., October 29, 1964, a commentary which concludes with the hope that West German calculations "will not succeed because the leadership of the Chinese People's Republic is not interested in supporting West German monopoly capitalism."

political import of any new arrangement. More important, to generate real "pressure" on the Soviet Union a German-Chinese trade agreement would have to involve a very major effort to underwrite Chinese industrial development and hence also military potential. Such an undertaking is hardly possible now, without producing enormous strains on the German-American relationship, given the continued conflict between the United States and China. And of course the inherent economic obstacles to any single-handed Western effort to sustain the development of as large and backward a country as China are close to insuperable.

The net effect would be opposite from the one achieved by limited collaboration with East Europe. Since East Europe does not represent a hostile and competitive challenge to Moscow, closer contacts with the West can serve also to bring the West closer to Russia; Western and particularly German aid to China, Russia's growing challenger, would hardly induce in the Russians a pro-Western orientation. Thus if trade develops between Germany and China, as it well may for purely economic reasons, the Germans would be advised not to give it a political flavor or to strive to expand it artificially for political purposes.

A more difficult problem in the Russian attitude toward Germany is raised by the issue of military security. In facing it, certain basic facts must be recognized: Germany is now rearmed conventionally; it is not going to be disarmed; no one in the West would contemplate that task and it could not be undertaken without fragmenting the West. Thus all schemes advocating the military neutralization of West Germany are politically unrealistic. The Central European problem cannot be solved by drastic changes in the existing security structure —faulty and tense though it be—for the problem is basically a political one. The military situation is its consequence. Political changes will have to precede the military changes; and political changes, as both sides have now learned, can only come gradually. The creation of a "neutral" or disengaged vac-

uum through the cooperative efforts of the two adversary superpowers (leaving aside its general improbability, given West
German and even French opposition to it),* would simply
mean the creation of new "hunting grounds" for the two opposed sides, unless that step was *preceded* by profound changes
in their political goals. By that time the scheme would no
longer be necessary.

Rejecting disengagement is not tantamount to standing
pat on the present division of Europe, nor does it justify the
argument that only the development of a militarily powerful
West Europe should be the object of American foreign policy.
The legitimate Western interest in the further development of
German defensive forces ought not to obscure the fact that
under certain circumstances it may increase the Soviet military
stake in East Germany. Again, this is not a matter for "either-
or" solutions. It is now probably idle to speculate whether
Germany should have been denied rocket weapons or kept
entirely out of the nuclear club (especially given the complications of the Franco-American rivalry). However, the possibility should not be excluded that, in view of the historically
founded Russian fear of Germany,† under certain conditions

* "For us, Central Europe is vital because it is a matter of life and death. It is
a question of our survival. We think that neutrality would be a great danger in Central Europe, because neutrality means a vacuum, and it would be a vacuum between the immense mass of Soviet military might and what would be left of
Western Europe, that is, France, the Benelux countries, and Italy." M. Couve de
Murville, Interview, *U.S. News and World Report*, March 16, 1964. American
disengagement from Europe would also be politically self-defeating, "for nothing
thrusts Germans more rapidly toward a Gaullist view of the world—or toward
thoughts of a deal of their own with Russia—than fear of American disengagement from Europe." (Robert Kleiman, *op. cit.* p. 146.) For a good review of the
various disengagement plans, see E. Hinterhoff, *Disengagement*, London, 1959.
More recently, some warmed-over versions of the plan rested on the premise that
the American role in Europe is finished and that a joint Soviet-American disengagement would restore both European stability and unity. (For example, see the
somewhat obscure and pontificating attack on NATO by Ronald Steel, *The End
of Alliance*, New York, 1964.)
† In this connection, there is an illusion shared by some that West German military
build up may someday become a useful basis for a deal with the Soviet Union:
East Germany for the denuclearization of West Germany. The fact is, however,
that the development of armed forces creates a vested interest. Subsequently it
becomes inconceivable that these forces be sacrificed, *in toto* or even in part, in

it might be desirable for Germany to limit its further military build up.

It is therefore not too late to note that the cause of German reunification is not likely to be served by the development of an independent German national nuclear force. To the extent that the Russians and the East Europeans strongly suspect that the MLF—or some Atlantic nuclear force—is a giant step precisely in that direction, it is in the interest both of the United States and West Germany to disabuse them of that impression. Accordingly the United States might be well advised to reiterate formally and explicitly the position taken in this regard by President Kennedy in his *Izvestia*, November 1961, interview. Germany might also derive political advantages from filing a formal declaration with the United Nations to the effect that under no circumstances will it seek an independent nuclear deterrent outside of multilateral control and management.*

Similarly, more thought should be given to the political implications of providing West Germany with rockets capable of striking directly at the Soviet Union. While still subject to the "two-key" system of control, the availability of such rockets to the West German armed forces brings Russia directly within reach of German striking power for the first time since World War II. This cannot but intensify Russian, Polish, and Czech feelings that a divided Germany is preferable to a united one. In this situation West Germany stands to lose little—and perhaps to gain a great deal—by repeatedly offering to con-

---

return for Soviet political concessions, because then the argument is raised that unity is purchased at the price of dependence. Since in the meantime the Soviet defensive stake in East Germany would have been increased, rearmament as a bargaining device is an illusion.

It is also wrong to think that the U.S. might be able to trade German participation in the MLF or in nuclear planning for Soviet concessions. Nothing is more likely to undermine Western confidence in American protection than the thought that Western collective security measures may be subject to bilateral American-Soviet negotiations.

* See my "Moscow and the MLF: Hostility and Ambivalence," *Foreign Affairs*, October 1964. This suggestion was subsequently advocated also by Senator J. W. Fulbright in November 1964.

clude bilateral nonaggression treaties with the East European states and by reiterating past pledges never to use force against the security and territorial integrity of its neighbors.

Our military policy should always strive to meet three basic requirements: to provide an adequate defense of West Europe; to develop a satisfactory distribution of responsibility in order to cope with the political problems of the Alliance; and, without sacrificing either of the preceding, to avoid a negative political feedback to the East. The last consideration has been most often neglected, even though it has become all the more important since the West is now increasingly inclined to bank on the promotion of evolutionary changes in the East. In our preoccupation with Western security we often tend to forget that the world looks quite different from the Russian and East European perspective, and that the history and psychology of the adversary must be taken into account, especially when our policy has as its ultimate objective the peaceful resolution of existing differences and a peaceful change in the status quo.

It cannot be stressed too often that no basic change in the division of Germany can be expected until the Russians and the East Europeans are prepared to accept the reunification of Germany. Such acceptance will require at some point a qualitative change in their outlook. The way to it is by gradual, marginal steps, carefully calculated to bring about a situation in which Moscow and the East Europeans will discover, as they did with Austria in 1955, that they no longer have any stake in East Germany.*

At this stage the basic preconditions for a German reuni-

* Those who advocate the development of the power of the West without much regard for its impact on the East inadvertently perpetuate the division of Germany. See for example, Dean Acheson, "Withdrawal from Europe? An Illusion," *The New York Times Magazine,* December 15, 1963. That is also why the opposite point of view as expressed by George Kennan, namely, that East Germany should at least transitionally be accepted ("Polycentrism and Western Policy," *Foreign Affairs,* January 1964) is also undesirable. Formal acceptance of the status quo would inevitably prompt dissension among the West Germans and the Americans and permit the Russians to have their cake and eat it too.

fication involving neither a communist take-over (a maximum Soviet goal) nor a unilateral Soviet pullout (a maximum Western goal) can be outlined only in very general terms:

i. The Soviet position in East Europe must have eroded to the point that the East European states are no longer pliant tools and East Germany has become an isolated Soviet colony, dependent entirely on Soviet garrisons. It is clearly within the power of the United States and West Germany to exert some influence to bring this condition into being.

ii. Poland and Czechoslovakia, at least on the broad popular level, must have ceased to view Germany as a territorially revisionist power. They must no longer feel the need of a Soviet presence in East Germany and must have ceased to be responsive to Soviet manipulation of the German bogey. Here, too, the West can exert influence by providing explicit guarantees of East European national and territorial integrity.

iii. The Soviet Union and the East European states must have been guaranteed that East Germany, once united with the rest of the country, will not become an outpost of NATO. This the West could certainly promise in advance. For example, commitments and arrangements could be made for an agreed period of time to keep East Germany a demilitarized area. While one German government would exercise sovereignty in all of Germany, only the present western part would remain in NATO (assuming the organization still existed), while in the present eastern part U.N. peace-keeping forces would temporarily be stationed. From the Soviet point of view, a more acceptable alternative might involve the transitional retention for some years of Soviet garrisons in East Germany, even though the country would have been reunited under one political authority (in effect, the Austrian precedent). The residual Polish and Czech fears of Germany would provide reassurance to Moscow that a new *cordon sanitaire* was not being created on its frontiers.

iv. The economic benefits now flowing from East Germany to CEMA and to the Soviet Union must be maintained.

This too is within the power of the West to assure. East Germany, as already noted (p. 81), is the Soviet Union's principal economic partner, and the Soviet Union's economic stake in East Germany is considerable. Substitute arrangements could be made bilaterally by Germany, or if such should develop, within a broader framework of European economic cooperation. However, for all of this to happen, more general changes in the East-West economic relationship will be required.

4. *To relate the expansion of economic ties to more extensive cultural and social contacts.* In the expansion of East-West trade, the West should attempt to erode the narrow ideological perspectives of the ruling communist elites and to prevent them from restricting closer contact exclusively to the economic realm, thus resolving their economic difficulties while consolidating their power and perpetuating the present partition of Europe. The communist leaders, with their public pleas for closer commercial relations (including Western credits), have been successful in representing themselves as the apostles of international cooperation. Western statesmen should be as vocal in stressing that concrete improvements in cultural relations, more intellectual dialogue and freedom of expression are as important as trade in creating genuine international cooperation. The two should always be related in every Western statement, comment, or negotiation with the East.

The economic situation in East Europe, and to a lesser extent in the Soviet Union, has arrived at a rather critical point in the last few years. These countries want closer economic relations with the West and in some cases large credits from the West. This makes East-West trade a potential Western asset. It should be used to advantage. Those in the West who oppose the expansion of such trade on the grounds that it helps the communist governments overlook the fact that, first, such trade will grow in spite of American objections and that, second, to the extent that such trade and credits are badly needed by the communists, they can be useful as sources of leverage.[3]

The communist leaders have made it plain that they see in the eventual economic superiority of their system the way to victory. Helping their economic development can be justified only if it produces such other consequences as the erosion of the communist commitment to domination, structural reforms in the communist economic systems, the growth of closer contacts, and an increasingly free flow of ideas and people.

These changes will not take place spontaneously, but as a result of steady pressure. Economic difficulties in the East stimulate intense power conflicts and thus tend to loosen the communist structure. It should not be forgotten that the strongest impulses toward liberalization—the Malenkov period in Russia and the later Khrushchev period of economic decentralization, the first Nagy period in Hungary and the recent reforms in Czechoslovakia—came because there were severe economic crises. They strengthened the hand of those who argued on behalf of liberalizing the system; they undermined the position of those who wished to avoid making a choice between political totalitarianism and economic reforms. It is no accident that, according to many observers, foreign trade officials of the communist countries are foremost among those who advocate structural economic reforms. An indiscriminate Western approach to trade and credits merely plays into the hands of those ruling communist officials who would like to avoid making substantial internal changes.*

Precisely because acceptance of Western aid and development of trade with the West is no longer proscribed as heretical by the communists, the West needs to define for itself a clearer political perspective on East-West trade. It will not do to view

---

* Giving aid to individual communist states and letting them use it as they see fit is exactly what Molotov proposed in 1947, in response to the Marshall Plan invitation. It was unacceptable then and there is no reason to feel that it should be acceptable now. For details, see Harry B. Price, *The Marshall Plan and Its Meaning*, Ithaca, 1955.

it, as otherwise conservative and staunchly anticommunist
businessmen often do, as merely an opportunity for profit-
making, the more so because once the gates have been opened
it becomes increasingly difficult to control economic appetites.
Accordingly, advance precautions will have to be taken to preserve the political perspective. Perhaps trade can be considered a purely economic issue when it takes place spontaneously, on the basis of reciprocal needs and advantages of the
trading parties. But when such trade has to be artificially stimulated by Western governments, when such trade is fostered
in the context of continued political and ideological conflict,
and when the Western businessmen who wish to extend credits
to the East at the same time desire their governments to underwrite these credits, such commercial relations cease to be
purely economic. As Abram Bergson, Professor of Economics
and Director of the Russian Research Center at Harvard, put
it in a report to the Senate Committee on Foreign Relations,
"U.S. policy in this area must be formulated primarily with
reference to political aspects." [4]

In very broad terms, American economic assistance
policy with respect to East Europe should be guided by two
basic criteria: whenever a country increases the scope of its
external independence from Soviet control, it should be rewarded; whenever a country appreciably liberalizes its domestic system, it should be rewarded. And similarly whenever
an opposite trend develops, the United States should be prepared to discontinue its assistance, withdraw special privileges,
such as the most-favored-nation clause (a matter of vital importance to the East Europeans), and should not hesitate
to indicate the political motivations involved. Given East
Europe's acute need for foreign capital investment, the flexible
use of American long-term credits in this regard could be an
important source of leverage.

That is why it is cause for regret that the United States
Congress has been so rigid with regard to the most-favored-
nation clause and to the application of Public Law 480 to

communist countries. Legislative restrictions on economic policy toward the communist states automatically restrict the power of the executive to negotiate with the communist states. Increasing the executive's room for maneuver would increase its ability to demand concessions from the communist states in exchange for more trade and credit. As things stand now, the communists, and particularly the Soviets, can publicly accuse the United States of restricting trade and Washington is unable to respond by inviting them to negotiate on this issue. This is a hindrance to effective conduct of foreign policy. Furthermore, dependence on Congress to exercise negative economic sanctions denies American policy-makers the flexibility and the freedom of timing that is necessary in the use of economic leverage. Congressional opinion tends to be slow in recognizing changes in the communist world, whereas promptness in responding to change and to opportunity is of the essence. A share of the blame for this Congressional rigidity, however, rests with the executive branch. Had it demonstrated earlier not only its capacity to use economic leverage positively, whenever favorable developments in the East warranted it, but also its willingness to use them *negatively*, i.e., to withdraw such privileges whenever retrograde trends in the East called for such action, some Congressional suspicion at least might have been allayed.*

Of course, it is difficult to turn economic relations on and off like a spigot. Applied too obviously, such leverage could become self-defeating, making trade relations with the West seem undesirable to the East European countries. Furthermore, it would be pointless to react to every unfavorable domestic turn in East Europe, given its political flux, by turning on the economic pressures. Indeed, there is some long-range advantage in developing a relatively stable level in trade

---

* However, the use of surplus food for this purpose is ill-advised, for it creates the impression that the United States is playing politics with people's hunger. The U.S. would be wise to avoid making surplus food the principal commodity extended to countries the U.S. wishes to influence politically. Once granted, it becomes almost impossible to withdraw (e.g., our difficulties with Nasser).

relations with East Europe as that inescapably helps to widen the range of its contacts with the West. However, to the extent that the United States and West Europe are in a position to grant special favors, for example, long-term credits or the most-favored-nation treatment, their extension to East European nations should periodically be reviewed from the standpoint of their over-all political utility.

In contrast to East Europe, it is difficult at the present to see any political advantage in granting long-term credits to the Soviet Union. The West has no political interest in promoting Soviet economic development or indirectly subsidizing Soviet economic aid programs, designed to reduce Western influence and to increase Soviet prestige in the developing countries, not to mention Soviet arms exports and efforts to encourage subversion. The argument that "a fat communist is a good communist" is too patently specious to be taken seriously. One need only speculate what the Soviet attitude would be if the United States needed Soviet credits for its further economic development and what conditions the Soviet Union would try to impose on the United States. Therefore, limits on long-term credits to the Soviet Union should be maintained. Exceptions could be granted in special cases when Western economic considerations warrant a departure from the established policy, but it would probably be advisable to adopt the position that private enterprises which are permitted under special circumstances to extend longer-term credits to the Soviet Union do so at their own risk without government guarantees.

Exceptions to this general rule might also be made when specific concessions, desirable from a political point of view, can be obtained in return. This may apply also more generally to the East European states, even when the basic criteria for granting credits are otherwise not met. The probability of obtaining substantial concessions should not be exaggerated. It would be idle to tie our willingness to expand trade with the communist states to excessive and unrealistic political conditions. But this does not mean that we should move to the other extreme and take the position that trade is by definition "neutral," and that it has no political implications. The recently concluded trade agreements between West Germany and some of the East European states demonstrate that marginal political concessions can be sought and obtained in exchange for trade. The West Germans were wise not to demand too much; for example, a rupture of relations with the Ulbricht regime.

Marginal concessions which could be sought in exchange for a liberalized trade policy and for Western credits include rules governing access to Berlin, to minimize Soviet opportunities for mischief making; binding and applicable consular agreements with all the communist states; the admission and free circulation of the Western press; more extensive and less regimented cultural exchanges; * and a relaxation of communist controls on travel of their citizens to the West.

To promote such travel, the United States and even more the West European nations, might be well advised to consider lifting existing visa restrictions, especially with regard to the East European youth. A scheme might be arranged which would allow East European students to be freely admitted for visits and which would make special arrangements to deal with their shortage of hard currency. For example, East Europeans could be permitted to exchange their currency at the frontier for convertible Western funds. The East European currency thus acquired could then be used by the West to finance common East-West undertakings designed to establish closer contacts: fellowships for worthy students, funds for West European tourists traveling in the East, highway systems, waterways, all of which would have the desirable effect of creating more multilateral bonds.

In the case of actual aid to the East European states, either by grants or credits, it is important that symbolic items

---

* A brief summary of American grievances against the Soviet handling of cultural exchanges is contained in S. Viederman, "Political Bars Hindering U.S.–Soviet Exchanges," *The New York Times,* January 13, 1965.

of a lasting nature be included. This facet of the problem has been almost entirely neglected. Few Russians remember today that millions of Russian lives were saved in the early twenties by the Hoover missions. Decades from now few Egyptians may remember the free distribution of American food, but the Russian-built Aswan dam will remind them of Russian aid. Accordingly, at least some of the assistance extended ought to be earmarked for undertakings which represent a lasting investment in popular goodwill. For example, the reconstruction of the Royal Castle in Warsaw with American funds (like the Rockefeller-financed restoration of Versailles) would be a fitting symbol of American presence in Poland, contrasting favorably with the generally unpopular Soviet-built Stalin Palace of Culture that dominates the Warsaw skyline. Better yet, the offer to construct a modern housing district in the war-devastated Polish capital would certainly have a major impact, regardless of official response. Joint American-West German financing of such a scheme might be beneficial, in view of the desirability of healing the Polish-German hostility.* In Czechoslovakia or Hungary (should American credits be eventually extended to these countries) the offer to construct and operate schools of business administration and agriculture could have a real impact, in view of the present difficulties faced by the communist governments in these areas. Similar gestures elsewhere by the United States and the West European nations would provide symbolic proof of the West's desire to bridge the political and ideological partition of Europe.

Western scholarships have already made a considerable contribution to bringing closer together the intellectual communities of the two sides. In this connection it is important to make certain that American-financed scholarships for study in America—an opportunity most eagerly sought in the Eastern

---

* The American-built children's hospital in Cracow, scheduled for completion in 1966, is a good precedent. This venture, however, was conceived and executed by a private individual, who had to overcome enormous obstacles on both sides of the ocean.

states and one providing enormous personal prestige to the recipients—are not misused as awards for loyalty to the communist regimes and ideology. This danger is implicit in arrangements that leave the nominating process entirely in the hands of the communist governments concerned. Obviously, no communist government will permit foreign institutions to reward its political opponents. But a more systematic effort should be made in the West to identify those scholars and intellectuals who have demonstrated both creativity and intellectual integrity and to insist that Western-financed fellowships not be awarded on the basis of other criteria. Unfortunately, departures from this standard have occasionally occurred, with some demoralizing effects within the East European intellectual community. To the extent that the communist governments are gradually becoming more sensitive to their own public opinion, and to the extent that the intellectual community has been pressing for closer contacts with the West, we should become more vigorous in asserting our own standards, while continuously and openly insisting that closer economic contacts must be paralleled by closer and freer cultural relations.

A special issue arises with respect to the role of East European public opinion. The present diversity in the communist world has made the communist leaders more responsive to the attitudes of the people. It would be counterproductive to focus American policy on the goal of improving relations with the present governments and to abandon efforts both to inform and to shape East European public opinion. The trip Robert Kennedy made to Poland in 1964 provides an illustration of how relationships with the people can occasionally be established. It is incorrect to dismiss this as merely an empty gesture or to argue that it complicates relations with the governments in power. Cultivation of these relations, it should always be remembered, is a means to an end and not the end in itself. A certain amount of direct popular appeal is desirable in keeping alive pro-Western popular sentiment and in stimulating it anew. The communist leaders, especially Khrushchev, have done this in their trips to the West; there is no reason for Western leaders to be more reticent than they in appealing directly to the people.

This leads to a sensitive but important question concerning the utility of Radio Free Europe (RFE). RFE has played a major role in keeping the East Europeans informed of developments in the world and, more importantly, in their own countries. Indeed, in many respects the "thaw" of the fifties was prompted by various revelations concerning internal communist politics broadcast by RFE. In more recent times, RFE has kept East Europeans informed about the developing Sino-Soviet dispute and it has helped counteract the rather unpleasant and intense communist campaign designed to portray the assassination of President Kennedy as a right-wing conspiracy, allegedly protected from exposure with the complicity of the U.S. government.* Indeed, by its mere existence RFE limits the ability of the communist governments to select and distort the news, lest the Radio gain a wider listening audience.[5]

RFE's semiofficial status permits it to comment more freely on the internal developments in the East European states than is the case with the necessarily blander and more cautious VOA broadcasts. Since the maintenance of a critical public opinion is essential to the further evolution of the communist governments, this division of labor between RFE and VOA ought to be maintained. The same considerations apply to the differing roles performed by Radio Liberty and VOA broadcasts to Russia. Moreover, it is important that RFE

---

* For example, the Polish government went out of its way to facilitate the distribution in Poland of the J. Buchanan book, *Who Killed Kennedy*, while Polish journalists stationed in the U.S. fed the Polish public a steady diet of slanted interpretations, designed to reinforce the plot theory. The other communist states were also equally active in this regard. For a tasteless commentary on the assassination, including the observation that murder is a "quite frequent" method of removing political opponents in the U.S., see M. Rakowski, *Ameryka Wielopietrowa* (Warsaw, 1963), a book of impressions written by the author after having been invited to visit the U.S.

broadcasts be sensitive to the national interests of the listening audiences. The Warsaw government has been able to embarrass RFE because for a long time the broadcasts beamed to Poland ignored the Polish view on the Oder-Neisse question. Any curtailment of the freedom of such institutions as RFE or Radio Liberty to criticize *internal* communist affairs could only be contemplated in the face of evidence that a free press and radio have begun to function in the East. Short of that, the West would be depriving itself of a useful and indirect means of influencing the outlook of millions of East Europeans and even Russians.

5. *To promote multilateral ties with West Europe and East Europe.* As direct Soviet control wanes, as East European nationalism, even under communist leadership, reasserts itself, as the East-West dichotomy becomes less sharp, it should be an explicit goal of American policy to promote multilateral political and economic relations, lest East Europe—and even all of Europe—become Balkanized.

Closer multilateral European ties would eventually render untenable the present semitotalitarian East European regimes which thrive on isolation; involvement in all-European undertakings would dilute their ideology and would inhibit the tendency for some of them to become more autonomous national-communist technocratic dictatorships. A Rumanian-style external independence with a semi-Stalinist dictatorship at home is not enough; a Hungarian-style internal liberalization with almost complete external dependence on the Soviet Union is also not enough. The two processes should be linked, but the West cannot encourage that to happen from the positions of the cold war. That is why economic assistance should be employed, but with a long-range goal in mind. Had more of an effort been made in the early fifties to draw Yugoslavia into all-European activities, perhaps some of its recent drift toward more regimentation at home and closer identification with the communist world abroad might have been averted.

Therefore, in subsequent relations with states that have

nationally asserted themselves, it is essential to insist on their gradual internal liberalization and on the creation of more binding multilateral links with the developing European community. The response to such Western pressure is likely to be twofold: an effort to compromise and meet some Western demands; and, to prevent absorption by the West, an effort to avoid a complete break with Moscow. This would contribute to desirable evolutionary trends in the region as a whole, encouraging both more autonomy and evolutionary liberalization.

A policy of bilateral differentiation made political sense in a period when Soviet control in East Europe was solid, because it weakened Soviet hegemony. In a period of greater East European diversity, bilateral relations between individual East European states and the West cease to have the same desirable effect. And just as in the West multilateral economic relations became the first step on the long road toward a broader political solution, so in the East-West European relationship the beginnings of a multilateral economic approach could pave the way to an eventual political reconciliation. Economic assistance to the East European countries inevitably has to begin on a bilateral basis, in conjunction with the expansion of other relationships. However, it should be clear that it is neither in the interest of East Europe nor of Europe as a whole to assist the economic development of individual East European states entirely on a bilateral basis, for this will resolve neither their specific economic problems nor the basic political issues dividing Europe.

The time may have come for some consideration to be given to the creation of a special fund for underwriting multilateral East-West economic undertakings. Hungary, for example, has been eager to undertake common industrial projects with Western partners. The creation of a special fund to assist such endeavors would encourage greater economic multilateralism. American involvement could certainly be of importance here. Also, to the extent possible, the multilateral

West European institutions could make it a matter of policy to hire East European specialists now resident in large numbers in West Europe in order to train a cadre of East European "European technocrats." Similarly, the East European states should be invited to permit their surplus working force to participate in the European labor market. Some East European countries suffer from hidden unemployment, while France,* Switzerland, and Germany badly need labor and import it from afar. Greater East-West labor mobility could be beneficial to everyone and would tend to undermine the existing European division. The exposure of many thousands of East Europeans to West Europe would have in time a profound social and ideological effect on the East.

Some East European states are beginning to engage in limited regional cooperation outside of CEMA, the membership of which is determined ideologically and includes even Mongolia. This development also deserves Western encouragement. East European regional economic cooperation helps to overcome the national antipathies still very strong in the area, and inevitably will weaken Soviet political control. So far, the East European states have not taken advantage of the facilities of the World Bank and the International Monetary Fund. Other developing nations have derived great benefits from such assistance, which, unlike many bilateral arrangements, is given on a continuing, long-term basis. Perhaps widely publicized offers by the World Bank and the IMF to assist East European *regional* economic undertakings might encourage the communist governments to join the institutions and stimulate popular pressure on behalf of more regional ventures.†

* Although there is no official confirmation, there is reason to believe that France and Poland have begun to make some limited arrangements to import surplus Polish labor to France, in effect, reviving a traditional flow interrupted after World War II.

† In a stimulating article, "World Bank Credits," *Kultura* (Paris), 10/204/1964, W. A. Zbyszewski, from whom the above idea is derived, discusses the extensive long-term credits obtained by Spain in modernizing its railroad network and by India for its economic development, and proposes that Poland, Czechoslovakia,

As a preparatory measure, it would be desirable for Western multilateral economic organizations to review, from a more political perspective, the character of East-West economic relations. It has already been noted that the Common Market headquarters do not have a regular political planning organ. The creation of such an office, charged with responsibility for analyzing the long-range political implications for East Europe of West European economic development, should be undertaken without delay, before the Common Market is in a position to shape a common commercial policy.* The creation of such a political staff would be of great value in relating an eventual common commercial policy to desirable political ends. While not a member of the Common Market, there is no reason why the United States as an interested party should not encourage Brussels to consider taking this step.

On their side, the communist states eventually will have to abandon their ideologically motivated hostility toward Western multilateral economic organizations, and it is to be hoped that they will do so as economic relations between the East and West develop. To encourage such evolution the Western states, including the United States, should continue to urge them to join GATT (Chapter Two, p. 64) † and to

---

Hungary, and Rumania should formulate joint proposals for their further development, to be assisted by the World Bank and the IMF. The suggestion deserves further exploration.

* For example, the January 24, 1963, regulation of EEC limits the import of Eastern agricultural products to a maximum of 120% of the 1960–61 average; in addition, under the July 1, 1962, regulation special levies are imposed on certain agricultural items. The effect of the regulations has been more sharply felt in East Europe than in Russia (given the important role of agricultural exports in these countries), with negative political effects. For example, Polish egg exports to Italy dropped in 1964 to only 13% of the 1961–63 level; to West Germany, to 10% of the 1959–61 level. See M. Dyner, "Agricultural Export to the Common Market," *Zycie Gospodarcze,* October 25, 1964.

† However, under GATT rules the United States would be compelled to grant the communist states most-favored nation treatment, which under domestic law it is currently forbidden to do. (A waiver had been obtained earlier in the case of Czechoslovakia, which remained after 1948 an inactive GATT member, but it is less certain that new waivers could be obtained.) This highlights the issue of flexibility versus legislative restrictions, discussed on p. 155.

extend formal diplomatic recognition to the Common Market as a supranational Western institution. The designation of communist ambassadors to EEC would have considerable ideological significance: it would mean a change in a doctrinaire position. From a practical point of view it would mean that, on some issues, the communist states would be able to negotiate directly with EEC instead, as now is the case, of having to deal indirectly with the various member states. It would mean greater contacts with a major supranational European organization and hence it would have the effect of drawing the communist states into a more involved relationship with Europe.* Perhaps as a preliminary step, some third institution, such as the Ford Foundation, which has sponsored many East-West conferences, may find it desirable to sponsor special conferences on the subject of the Common Market to which Eastern European and Soviet economists would be invited.

A more flexible and less ideological communist attitude toward Western multilateralism may pave the way to other measures that could be economically beneficial to the communist states and could serve to unite Europe. Acceptance by the communist states of world prices as a basis for their domestic pricing system would facilitate multilateral trade, now in part inhibited by the arbitrary and incalculable communist pricing system. Consideration could be given to special arrangements providing for the accession of communist states to some sort of association with OECD, at least to the extent of inviting them to participate in particular phases of work that concern them. The advantages of East European participation in OECD would be several: 1) They would be allowed to take part in preliminary and private discussions of measures planned by member states which will affect states that do not belong to OECD. This would give them an

* Since EEC is a supranational organ and CEMA is not, communist diplomatic recognition of EEC should not be equated with Western recognition of CEMA. There is no formal or structural equivalence between the two.

indirect share in the economic decision making of greater powers. 2) They would benefit from a certain amount of pooling of information, both economic and technical, that is important for their economic planning and development. 3) They could take advantage of the limited technical assistance that OECD provides to less developed states. Some members of OECD have insisted on being categorized as less developed states so that they could benefit from such technical aid.* East European participation in OECD would thus symbolize the triumph of the Western conception of European multilateral development, while also benefiting the East European nations economically.

The development on a multilateral basis of economic relations between the East and the West could gradually pave the way for progress in the more sensitive field of politics. Progress in economic cooperation would lessen the fear of the East European ruling elites that the West intends to absorb the East European states one by one. It would work against the revival of historically retrogressive inner-oriented nationalist states. With progress in increasing economic, cultural, and human contacts, consideration could be given to steps on the political level. For example, the formation could be explored of a standing committee of prominent East and West Europeans, with Soviet and American participation, to examine periodically the state of East-West relations. A standing committee of this kind (modeled on the various groups and committees which have played so large a part in West European unification) would have an advantage over the occasional *ad hoc* bilateral and multilateral East-West conferences, for it could gradually develop into a working body with a profes-

* Finland, which for political reasons must be extremely careful not to offend the Soviet Union, participates in OECD through observers and specifically in regard to matters affecting its basic industries. Yugoslavia, which has recently become associated with CEMA, is a full member for confrontation of economic policies, scientific, and technological matters, agriculture and fisheries questions, technical assistance and productivity, and participates through observers in other matters. (See *OECD* [no date], Paris). Yugoslavia and Finland could both serve as useful precedents for the other East European states.

sional staff, in effect creating the first nucleus of functional all-European bodies.

Looking still further ahead, one can envisage periodic all-European conferences of chiefs-of-government. Here too both American and Soviet participation would be desirable. Formally their participation could be justified by their respective adherence to the Atlantic alliance and the Warsaw Pact. More basically, it would be required to maintain a political balance and to avoid the impression that European participation, without the Soviet Union and the United States, was designed to break the East European-Soviet and West European-American relationships. At first, such consultative gatherings would probably accomplish little. In time, they could become a useful forum for the consideration of all-European problems and, more important, for the development of a sense of a common European identity.

It is to be expected that the Soviet Union would wish to take advantage of any multilateral forum to enhance the status of its East German regime. In time, however, and with progress in the areas of policy already considered, it might be expected that not all the East European states would give Moscow complete and unilateral backing on that issue. Some of them may be tempted to become involved in all-European undertakings, even if it does mean that East Germany is excluded from them, provided some face-saving device could be found.

The development of multilateral ties also *within* East Europe would be desirable, both for its own sake and as a step toward a larger European community. Since much of the tragic history of East Europe can be traced to its internal divisions, there may be a special merit for the United States, which continues to enjoy unequaled prestige among the East European peoples,* to go on record as favoring the eventual

---

* Although in many places in the world the United States seems to have lost some of its hold on the popular imagination, in East Europe it is still seen in highly idealized terms as the society of tomorrow, a feeling strengthened by per-

formation of an East European confederation, thereby emulating the West European development. Historically all the foreign efforts to "organize" East Europe have been associated with hostile designs to dominate the region. But no one in East Europe could suspect hegemonistic designs on the part of the United States if, at some appropriate historic and symbolic occasion, the President were to outline in bold terms this country's hope for an East Europe that would rise above its traditional divisions and assume a more important role in shaping the future Europe. With the decline in Soviet control and with the weakening of the ideological commitment of the ruling East European elites, the resulting East European void could be filled by an idea that is in keeping especially with the widespread but often inarticulate aspirations of the younger generation to surmount the old divisions. Otherwise, there is the danger that as the communist elites become "nationalized," the old animosities will be rekindled and exploited by internal and external forces.

Such an American statement might be particularly timely because many East Europeans (including some officials) are concerned that the new American-Soviet stability may result in East Europe becoming again a backyard of international politics—an area to be occasionally exploited by the United States in order to put pressure on the Soviet Union, but otherwise left to its own devices and to the mercy of its more powerful neighbors, eventually including Germany. That is why a constructive statement defining the American hopes for the future development of East Europe would be much more than propaganda. Even if initially criticized by the communist press as interference, it would help give a new sense of direc-

---

sonal bonds with many millions of Americans of East European origin. Symptomatic of the feeling of the youth was the finding of a survey conducted in Warsaw during the communist May Day Youth Celebration: when asked where they would like to go if all restrictions were lifted, the universal answer was "America." See Z. Bauman, *Kariera*, Warsaw, 1960, p. 98, cited by *Tygodnik Powszechny*, July 5, 1964.

tion to many East Europeans who are concerned about their future but see no one providing them with a constructive alternative to the present.

From Confrontation to Cooperation

The American-Russian detente creates a propitious setting for a creative and dramatic act by the United States. Until now, most East-West agreements have been negotiated during periods of tension and crisis.[6] Since most of the crises were initiated by Soviet efforts to change the status quo, the initiative has tended to rest with Moscow. The settlements (with the exception of the Austrian Treaty and the Test Ban Agreement) involved the restoration of the previous situation. In the post-Cuba detente, there is a broader opportunity for the West to come to grips with the basic problem of East-West relations. By taking the initiative, America would point up the broader scope of America's European policy and accelerate the tendencies in the East which are favorable to closer East-West relations. The appropriate content of such an initiative would be economic, since that is the most vulnerable point in East Europe, and since the possibility of East-West economic cooperation has achieved a certain ideological respectability in East Europe.

To that end, the United States, speaking through its President, should address a proposal to the European powers, including Russia, to join with America in formulating a joint all-European economic development plan. The plan would be designed to cut across the present European partition, to narrow existing disparities in European living standards, to reduce the economic and political significance of existing frontiers, and to promote East-West trade and human contacts by the development of an all-European system of communications. The proposal would be a fitting climax to past American efforts to foster the unity of Western Europe, to bring about closer contacts between East and West, and in this context to build a stable relationship between Germany and East Europe. In the proposed plan, American financial participation would be conditional on complementary efforts by West Europe. The European Economic Community could participate as an entity by creating a special fund to finance East-West trade and common European investment projects, or by extending the scope and the size of its Development Fund and the European Investment Bank. Working out new trade agreements with the East in the context of a larger American-sponsored plan of East-West economic cooperation would also aid the process of West European unification.

A venture of this kind would take advantage of the West's economic strength, of economic pressures in the East, and of the growing appeal of the European idea in Eastern Europe in contrast to the waning attraction of communist ideology. There is reason to hope that West Europeans would be ready to make the contributions necessary to bring this collective enterprise into being. For example, a 1962 poll showed a large majority of the West Europeans in favor of using national taxes to promote the development of the poorer regions of Europe (while a small majority opposed the same for Africa).[7] That West Europe could contribute substantial capital is suggested by the present size of West German commitments to international development: $1,050 million to the capital stock of the International Bank for Reconstruction and Development, $200 million to the development fund of EEC, $300 million to the European Investment Bank. With contributions from the other Western European states and from the United States, a proposal of this kind would have a dramatic appeal in both Eastern and Western Europe.

The proposal would be premised on a phased reunification of Germany and on an implicit acceptance by the East of the principle that the reconstruction of Europe would involve in time the reunification of Germany. A general plan of European economic cooperation, involving multilateral Western participation and open both to Russia and to East Europe, would be more acceptable in the East than any bilateral attempt by West Germany "to buy" East Germany in exchange for credits to Russia, as has at times been proposed in the West German press and repeatedly rejected by the East.[8] A direct German-Russian relationship would create fears and opposition in East Europe, not to speak of suspicions of a new Rapallo in the West. Only a solution of the German problem in the context of broader East-West cooperation could reasonably assure both sides that reunification would not lead to the fragmentation of one side or the other.

No doubt the Soviet Union would try to take advantage of a proposal of this kind to legalize the existence of the two German states by insisting that East Germany should participate formally in any all-European undertaking. Yet it is by no means certain that, if the West takes the steps already suggested to reassure the East Europeans on the German question, the Soviet Union would be able to count on the solid support of the East European states. The idea of rejoining Europe would generate much popular enthusiasm in East Europe. The economic opportunity thereby presented would doubtless be attractive to the harassed East European economic cadres. The economic character of the proposal would diminish the suspicions of the political elites. Increasingly concerned with their own well-being, these governments might be receptive to a formula excluding East-German participation on the grounds that East Germany benefits already from advantageous bilateral economic arrangements with West Germany.

If actually launched, and in operation for a period of years, such unprecedented multilateral economic cooperation would sooner or later create a favorable context for resolving peacefully the many outstanding European political and security problems. In the new atmosphere, it might be possible to find solutions for the more intractable problems of arms control; to achieve perhaps a freeze on nuclear weapons; and even to explore again various regional security schemes. In the present hostile confrontation it is unavoidable that each side assumes that any security scheme proposed by the other has ulterior motives.

Of course, the Soviet Union might reject any such cooperative venture. Or, more likely, it would equivocate and attempt to shift the focus of the proposal to direct grants to individual communist states, thereby frustrating the underlying purpose of the initiative. Yet at least some of the East European states would surely be attracted, and there would be great popular pressure in East Europe for participation. It is by no means certain that a Soviet refusal would be automatically followed by East European refusals, as happened with the Marshall Plan. Indeed, one should not assume that the Soviets would continue indefinitely to reject it.

In assessing possible Soviet reactions, one must recognize that the general evolutionary trend in Russia toward a more European orientation is counterbalanced by increasing Russian nationalism and even chauvinism, and by the power interests of the bureaucratic-technocratic dictatorship which is likely to continue to dominate the Soviet political scene. It is quite possible that the ruling elite will seek to justify its power by emphasizing the global competition with the United States, building on the desire of many Russians to become the number one world power. It is therefore possible that the Soviets would be unwilling to participate in any scheme which appeared to involve eventual reunification of Germany and lessening of Russian control over East Europe. For this reason, American policy must reckon not only with the possibility of a favorable Soviet evolution, but also with the possibility of persisting Soviet hostility.

The proposed American initiative for all-European economic cooperation does just this. If the favorable Soviet evolution, foreseen in this study, comes to pass, the proposal opens the way for the Soviet Union and East Europe to move toward a grand settlement and reconciliation with the West. If Soviet hostility persists, the proposal would put increased strain on the Soviet control of East Europe. It would increase the cost of Soviet domination by giving the East Europeans new leverage to extract greater Soviet economic assistance in return for their rejecting the Western initiative. Thus, the initiative is desirable on either assumption about the trends of Soviet domestic development.

The United States would benefit politically by the mere fact of making the proposal. At the very least, it would give us an honest and rational policy on German reunification. Once made, the proposal would become an objective force, just as Khrushchev's bold disarmament proposals gave Soviet foreign policy a certain positive momentum, though they were never implemented. The initiative could mobilize the West and attract the East, irrespective of formal acceptances or refusals. Its positive appeal would doubtless create some division of opinion in Moscow and might help the moderate forces in Soviet society.

The reader will not have failed to note the historical connection between the proposal here made and the original proposal of the Marshall Plan. The immense political force of a far-reaching initiative, made at the right time, was never more clearly demonstrated. In the eloquent words of its chronicler, Harry Price:

"The Marshall Plan demonstrated that the free nations can seize the initiative in the East-West struggle if goals are set which exert a wide and potent appeal and if enough intelligence, energy, and resources are devoted to the attainment of these goals. . . .

"The Plan began with an idea. It was an idea which satisfied a widely felt yearning and fired the imagination and hopes of millions. Its conception and projection was a creative event. Yet the uniqueness of the concept was less extraordinary than its historic timing, the way in which it entered into and became a part of existing currents of thought and feeling. . . . To usher in a new era in relations between peoples—an era in which the energies released in cooperative enterprises eventually outstrip those dedicated to defense or destruction—not one or two ideas but a whole sequence of new concepts is needed. One of the lessons of the Marshall

Plan appears to be that for an idea to be effective in the international sphere, as has been true in the industrial sphere, it must be addressed to a situation that is ripe for it.[9]

Price describes in vivid terms the starkness of the European situation in 1947.[10] The Marshall Plan was born of the frustration and failure of the Moscow Conference and was designed to be "a broad and dramatic effort." Today, in the context of nuclear proliferation, the rise of West European nationalisms, the decline of United States influence on the European continent, the growing frustration in West Germany, and the increasing opportunities in the more divided East, there is again a need and an increasingly ripe historical opportunity for a bold and creative idea.

As long as the West is militarily strong and clear about its goals, we need not fear to extend to the communist world a sincere offer of economic cooperation designed neither to strengthen nor to weaken those who have made themselves our adversaries, but to bind us all together so that we can no longer consider warring against each other. Even in the darkest days of the forties, the policy planning staff of the State Department felt, and rightly so, that "American effort in the aid to Europe should be directed not to combating of communism as such, but to the restoration of the economic health and vigor of European society." [11] In that, it had the support of the American economic community.[12] It is more than likely that in the more hopeful context of the sixties, and especially after the 1964 American elections, the same support would be forthcoming.

Those who say that the New World no longer has any mission of relevance to the Old or that a Europe tied to America would be "soulless and rootless," are wrong. But only America can prove them wrong. America was highly relevant to a divided and insecure West Europe, faced by a united Soviet bloc. The idea of the Atlantic community was a creative and effective response to a challenging Russia. This is no longer the challenge we face. America is becoming irrelevant to a divided but secure West Europe, faced by an increasingly independent East Europe. In this new setting, the Atlantic idea alone is not an adequate response to Europe's quest for identity and to the opportunity presented by a weakening Soviet bloc.

The proposed initiative would have the merit of creating a larger context for continued American-European cooperation, sublimating the tendency for European unification processes to become also an expression of the European desire for divorce from the United States. Even if it did not succeed in reconciling the East and the West, it would nonetheless provide a common objective sufficiently important to support a positive American-West European relationship. A larger conception of a future cooperative community, involving eventually four major units, America and Russia as the peripheral participants, and West Europe and East Europe as the two halves of the inner core (in time perhaps becoming still more closely linked), would provide a more constructive and politically appealing image of tomorow than a troubled Western partnership implicitly based on the notion of continued European partition.

A broader conception, of which the Atlantic partnership could be one component, would be more likely to keep the United States relevant to Europe's future, to prevent the recrudescence in Europe of narrow nationalisms or the perpetuation of xenophobic national communisms, and to create a new political context in which the legacies of World War II could at last be settled. America could set itself no nobler or more timely task than seeking to end the partition of Europe.

Notes

CHAPTER ONE

1. For an account of its motives, including the decision by its sponsors and backers to make it open to East Europe and the Soviet Union, see H. B. Price, *The Marshall Plan and Its Meaning*, Ithaca, N.Y., 1955.

2. R. Kleiman, *The Atlantic Crisis*, New York, 1964, p. 23. For a fuller discussion of De Gaulle's politics, see R. Massip, *De Gaulle et l'Europe*, Paris, 1963.

3. For a French view of the Franco-German rapprochement, see René Lauret, *France and Germany*, Chicago, 1964. For evidence of declined Franco-German popular hostility, see the report by Gallup International on "Public Opinion and the European Community," *Journal of Common Market Studies*, November 1963.

4. For a very extensive analysis of European public opinion toward the issue of European unity, the Common Market, the advantages and disadvantages of closer ties, see *Sondages* (Revue Française de l'opinion publique), No. 1, 1963, devoted to the European issue. (It also contains interesting data on the extent of inter-European travel in the West, which stands in sharp contrast to the continued parochialism of the East. See Chapter Two.)

5. For extensive analyses, see J. Freymond, *Western Europe Since the War*, New York, 1964. The most that the communist elites could do was to organize formal, bureaucratically-controlled, bilateral "friendship societies" that would meet on the various national anniversaries and extol each others' five-year plans.

6. For conflicting views regarding continued Soviet economic discrimination, see Horst Mendershausen, "Terms of Trade Between the Soviet Union and Smaller Communist Countries 1955–57," *Review of Economics and Statistics*, Vol. 41 (May 1959), pp. 106–118; "The Terms of Soviet Satellite Trade: A Broader Analysis," *op. cit.*, Vol. 42 (May 1960), pp. 152–163; and Franklyn D. Holzman, "Soviet Foreign Trade. Pricing and the Question of Discrimination," *op. cit.*, Vol. 44 (May 1962), pp. 134–147. The exchange continued in the "Notes and Book Reviews" section of the *Review*, Vol. 44 (November 1962), pp. 493, 496, 499.

7. *Memoires de Guerre*, Vol. II, *L'Unité 1942–44*, Paris, 1956–59, p. 98.

8. G. Malenkov, *Pravda*, October 6, 1952.

9. *Kommunist*, No. 14, 1955, p. 127.

10. A useful summary is in J. B. Thompson, "Rumania's Struggle with Comecon," *East Europe*, June 4, 1964. For economic roots, see J. M. Montias, "Background and Origins of the Rumanian Dispute with Comecon," (mimeographed, 1964).

11. *Problems of Peace and Socialism*, September 1962.

12. M. Gamarnikow, "Comecon Today," *East Europe*, March 1964.

13. I. Rachmuth, "The Importance of Establishing a Rate of Development Which

Will Level Off the Economic Progress of All Socialist Countries," *Probleme Economice,* Bucharest, July 1963.

14. Letter of the Central Committee of the CPC to the Central Committee of the CPSU, dated February 29, 1964.

15. *Pravda,* September 2, 1964.

16. *Neues Deutschland,* April 18, 1964.

17. Radio Budapest, May 19, 1964.

18. For a good over-all account, see Z. A. Jordan, "The Ideologies of Polish Youth: From Revolution to Withdrawal," *East Europe,* January 1964.

19. E.g., the four shutdowns in 1963–64 of more liberal magazines. (The latest case reported in *The New York Times,* June 13, 1964.)

20. On exaggerating the role of the peasantry, see *Pravda,* May 11, 1964, "What Are the Chinese Leaders Foisting on the Communist Movement Under the Guise of Marxism-Leninism?". On the necessity of condemning "the theory of violence," see P. Fedoseyev, "Materialist Understanding of History and 'The Theory of Violence,'" *Kommunist,* May 1964. Both were authoritative ideological statements. For an able over-all treatment, see R. Lowenthal, *World Communism,* New York, 1964.

21. The theory is developed extensively in the speech by Chou Yang, "The Fighting Task of Workers in Philosophy and in the Social Sciences," *Peking Review,* no. 1 (January 3), 1964, pp. 10–27.

22. R. V. Vyatkin and S. L. Tikhvinski, "Some Questions of Historical Science in the Chinese People's Republic," *Voprosy Istorii,* No. 10, October 1963.

23. See the very revealing data in S. Bialer, "The Soviet Elite," a Ph.D. dissertation in progress, Columbia University.

24. E.g., N. Khrushchev's attacks on the intellectuals "who had succumbed to bourgeois ideology" and his declaration against "peaceful coexistence in ideology," especially his speech of March 8, 1963.

25. For comments, see B. Bogunovic, "With Whom and Against Whom?", *Borba,* February 29, 1964. For some East German reactions, fearful of Chinese-West German cooperation, see *Neues Deutschland,* May 14, 1964.

CHAPTER TWO

1. A very useful summary is contained in the report compiled by A. Stypulkowski and others on East-West cultural relations, prepared for the European Movement (Brussels, mimeographed, 1963).

2. *Ibid.,* pp. 10–13 for an extensive listing of these relations.

3. *Trybuna Ludu,* June 17, 1964.

4. D. Nemes, "On Some Timely Questions Connected with the International Communist Movement," *Nepszabadsag,* June 5, 1964.

5. *Le Monde,* July 2–8, 1964, citing the report of M. Hertzog, responsible for the Franco-German Youth Office.

6. See *Ceteka,* February 11, 1964, and the RFE Background Report on *The Manpower Crisis in Czechoslovakia,* June 13, 1964 (citing *Ceteka* and other Czech sources).

7. A. Rajkiewicz, "Employment—A Problem Which Is Not Merely Economic," *Nowe Drogi,* June 1964.

8. Nemes, *op. cit.*

9. This is openly admitted by a Soviet analyst, I. N. Beliaev, *"SEV i 'obshchii rynok,'"* Moscow, 1964, pp. 33–34.

10. For a full account of the application of the Mutual Defense Assistance Control Act of 1951 [The Battle Act], see the report to Congress by Secretary of State Dean Rusk, *The Battle Act Report 1964*, Seventeenth Report to Congress, Department of State, Washington, D.C., 1964. See particularly pp. 37–39 for a list of banned items of indirect military value.

11. E.g., see H. J. Kirchner, "The New German-Polish Trade Agreement," *Europa-Archiv*, No. 7, 1963, for a comprehensive review.

12. For a detailed treatment, see G. Chernikov, "Economic Collaboration between France and the USSR: Traditions and Perspectives," *Mirovaia Ekonomika i Mezhdunarodnie Otnosheniia*, No. 3, 1960, pp. 15–28.

13. V. Pavlat, "EEC and East-West Trade," *Mirovaia Ekonomika i Mezhdunarodnie Otnosheniia*, No. 11, 1963.

14. See the very detailed country by country breakdown, including lists of commodities traded, compiled in the unclassified research monograph, *Trade of NATO Countries with the Communist Countries, 1960–62*, Department of State, Washington, 1964.

15. *Annual Economic Indicators for the U.S.S.R.*, Materials prepared for the Joint Economic Committee, Congress of the United States, February 1964, p. 113.

16. The preceding discussion benefited from the interesting polemical article by W. A. Zbyszewski, "The Common Market and Eastern Europe," *Kultura* (Paris), June 1964.

17. *The New York Times*, June 29, 1964; London UPI, July 13, 1964.

18. *Le Monde*, June 18–24, 1964.

19. For systematic analysis of the decline in the standard of living in Czechoslovakia, see V. Holesovsky, *Personal Consumption in Czechoslovakia, 1937, 1948–1960*, unpublished Ph.D. thesis, Department of Economics, Columbia University, 1964. For East-West German comparisons, see *The Bulletin*, May 19, 1964. For Czech expressions of concern over the abortion rate, see *Mlada fronta*, February 4, 1961; *Prace*, June 21, 1961. For a review of the Hungarian population crisis, *Le Monde*, May 21–27, 1964.

20. S. Kurowski, *Historyczny proces wzrostu gospodarczego*, Warsaw, 1963.

21. E.g., see the review of it in *Survey*, No. 51, April 1964, pp. 148–152, "The Advantages of Backwardness," by A. Brzeski.

22. Kurowski, *op. cit.*, pp. 132–133.

23. *Ibid.*, pp. 170–175.

24. *Ibid.*, p. 335.

25. For some comparative data, see my "The Soviet Bloc, the Common Market and France," in S. Fisher, ed., *France and the European Community*, Ohio University Press, 1965; also, "Economic Development and the Comecon Countries," *Planovane Hospodarstvi*, April 1964.

26. See the analyses of L. Smolinski, "What Next in Soviet Planning?," *Foreign Affairs*, July 1964, and M. Gamarnikow, "The Growth of Economic Revisionism," *East Europe*, May and July 1964.

CHAPTER THREE

1. This case is developed more fully in my "Cuba in Soviet Strategy," *The New Republic*, November 3, 1962.

2. See the broad assessment of the year 1963, "Current Problems of World Politics," *Mirovaia Ekonomika i Mezhdunarodnie Otnosheniia*, No. 1, January 1964, p. 10; V. Matveyev, "Western Europe: Asset or Liability in the Struggle for Peace?", *International Affairs*, January 1963, p. 56.

3. Matveyev, *op. cit.*, p. 56.

4. *Economic Bulletin for Europe*, Vol. XV, No. 1, p. 25.

5. D. Mel'nikov, "A Threat to European Security," *International Affairs*, March 1957, pp. 46–65.

6. I. Chelnokov, "The European Coal and Steel Community," *International Affairs*, February 1957, pp. 94–104.

7. Mel'nikov, *op. cit.*

8. Quite typical is V. Khyazhinsky, "United Europe, A Weapon of Imperialist Policy," *International Affairs*, June 1957, pp. 51–58.

9. Characteristic is the commentary by V. Cherpakov, "The Common Market— An Instrument for the Intensification of Monopolistic Oppression and Aggression," *Kommunist*, May 1962, pp. 22–35.

10. E.g., I. Lemin, "European Integration: Some Results and Perspectives," *Mirovaia Ekonomika i Mezhdunarodnie Otnosheniia*, April 1962, pp. 21–36.

11. Some Soviet observers now went as far as to negate their previous warnings about "German hegemony" and talked about "French hegemony in Western Europe." For example, see Lemin, *op. cit.*, Part II, May 1962, pp. 42–55; and Cherpakov, *op. cit.*

12. For a good example of such conflicting motivations, see Viktor Mayevsky's correspondence from England, *Pravda*, August 29, 1962.

13. *New Times* (Moscow), January 30, 1963.

14. See the cautious statement in the annual round up, published by *Mirovaia Ekonomika i Mezhdunarodnie Otnosheniia*, No. 1, 1964, p. 12. For a more vigorous emphasis on contradictions designed for public consumption, see the round-table discussion by leading Soviet commentators, Radio Moscow, December 22, 1963.

15. *The New York Times*, May 6, 1964.

16. That is the dominant theme of the collective volume on the Common Market edited by V. S. Zorin and E. P. Pletnev, *'Obshchi rynok'—Orudie Monopolii*, Moscow, 1963. For a fuller discussion, see my "Europe and Russia," *Foreign Affairs*, April 1964.

17. Contrast the glowing praises of neutralism in Khrushchev's speech to the Norwegians (*Pravda*, July 1, 1964) with the arguments against neutralism for Hungary advanced by Politburo member G. Kallai (*Nepszabadsag*, June 26, 1964) in response to French left-wing suggestions that a neutral Hungary could be "a bridge" between the East and the West.

18. See, for example, the perceptive analysis of J. Mieroszewski, "Poland-Germany-America," *Kultura* (Paris) February 1964. Mieroszewski is a leading Polish exile specialist in international affairs.

19. Alard von Schack, "Alternatives to the Polish Policy toward Germany," *Aussenpolitik*, November 1963.

20. For some conflicting German points of view, see von Schack, *op. cit.,* and (for a rather qualified defense of the Hallstein doctrine) W. Zoll, "On the Value of the Hallstein Doctrine," *Aussenpolitik,* September 1963; and a more vigorous but typically legalistic defense, R. Schuster, "The Hallstein Doctrine," *Europa-Archiv,* No. 18, 1963.

21. *Frankfurter Allgemeine Zeitung,* February 1, 1957.

22. Stenzl, *op. cit.,* p. 124.

23. Based on the detailed and documented version in Stenzl, *op. cit.*

24. *Le Monde,* citing his interview in *Die Zeit,* April 7, 1962.

25. For an earlier indication of Schroeder's thoughts, see his comprehensive piece on "Basic Problems of the Foreign Policy of the Federal Republic of Germany," *Europa-Archiv,* No. 17, 1962.

26. For a substantive analysis providing the broader framework for it, see Helmut Allardt, "Germany and Poland," *Aussenpolitik,* May 1963. Dr. Allardt headed the German delegation that signed the Polish-German trade agreement. In his article the author criticizes past German efforts to dismember Poland and advocates diplomatic relations, leaving aside the problem of frontiers. See also, E. W. Meyer, "Steps towards Reunification and towards Peace," *Aussenpolitik,* September 1963.

27. *Neues Deutschland,* April 16, 1964.

28. Radio Prague, June 21, 1964.

29. For a forceful and able statement of such views, see A. Dalma of Munich in the paper "Central Europe in the Context of Changing East-West Relations," (mimeographed) presented to the colloquium on "Changing East-West Relations and the Unity of the West," of the Washington Center for Foreign Policy, May 1964, esp. pp. 8, 13, and 20. Dalma is a leading German specialist in international affairs and a close associate of Franz-Josef Strauss.

30. For example, P. Coulmas, "Creating a Detente: Motives, Illusions, and Boundaries," *Aussenpolitik,* January 1964, defends the Hallstein doctrine and the non-recognition of the Oder-Neisse line and argues that giving them up would bring closer the attainment of the communist goal of world domination. For a broader statement, echoing this position, see Baron T. von und zu Guttenberg, *Wenn der Westen Will,* 1964.

31. For a perceptive and sympathetic review of De Gaulle's policy, see Stanley Hoffmann, "De Gaulle, Europe, and the Atlantic Alliance," *International Organization,* No. 1, 1964. For a devastating critique, Paul Reynaud, *La Politique Étrangère du Gaullisme,* Paris, 1964.

32. Speech in Lyons, September 28, 1963.

33. Press Conference of July 29, 1963.

34. Interview with the French Foreign Minister, *U.S. News and World Report,* March 16, 1964.

35. De Gaulle, March 17, 1964.

36. Address by Premier G. Pompidou, February 24, 1964.

37. De Gaulle, December 31, 1963.

38. Press Conference March 25, 1959.

39. A. Kawalkowski, "For a Europe Independent and Reunified," *Politique Étrangère,* No. 3, 1963.

40. May 15, 1962.

41. In the spring of 1964 *Le Monde* subjected the "force de frappe" to withering critique, notably by the Club Jean Moulin.

42. *Le Monde*, July 23–29, 1964.

43. See his press conference of March 25, 1959.

44. Typical in this regard were the views of Paul Henri Spaak. For his criticisms of the Franco-German pact, see *Neues Zürcher Zeitung*, May 18, 1963.

45. For a fuller critique, see my "United States Foreign Policy in East Central Europe," *Journal of International Affairs*, No. 1, 1957.

46. *Report on Exchanges with the Soviet Union and Eastern Europe*, No. 21, July 1, 1963, Department of State, Washington, D.C.

47. For a vigorous and well-reasoned case against extending aid to these countries, see Milorad Drachkovitch, *United States Aid to Yugoslavia and Poland*, Washington, 1963.

48. For a fuller elaboration of the new approach, see Z. Brzezinski and W. E. Griffith, "Peaceful Engagement in Eastern Europe," *Foreign Affairs*, July 1961.

49. For a similar statement, see the French communist comments on the Soviet-Chinese dispute in *Les Temps Modernes, op. cit.*, esp. p. 1993.

50. For a criticism of the earlier position, see my "The Danger of a German Veto," *The New Leader*, January 20, 1964.

51. See the two articles by Herbert von Borsch, "The Anatomy of a Dissention," *Aussenpolitik*, June 1962, and "America and the European Status Quo," *Aussenpolitik*, February 1964.

52. J. P. Smith, *The Defense of Berlin*, Baltimore, 1963, p. 333. See also *The New York Times*, April 14 and 15, 1962.

53. *The New York Times*, April 17, 1962.

54. For lengthier West German commentary, see Manfred Ablein, "The Negotiations over the Internationalization of the Approaches to Berlin since the Fall of 1961," *Europa-Archiv*, No. 12, 1963.

CHAPTER FOUR

1. Brzezinski and Griffith, *op. cit.*

2. See note, p. 103.

3. See in this connection a very persuasive plea for using trade as a political weapon by Hans J. Morgenthau, "Peace in Our Time?", *Commentary*, March 1964.

4. Committee on Foreign Relations, U.S. Senate, *East-West Trade, A Compilation of Views of Businessmen, Bankers, and Academic Experts*, November 1964, p. 224.

5. For an example of East European cynicism with regard to their own press and radio, see the story in *The New York Times*, May 5, 1964.

6. Dallin, *op. cit.*, p. 190.

7. See "Public Opinion and the European Community," *Journal of Common Market Studies*, November 1963, p. 115.

8. *Die Welt*, July 3, 1964; *Der Stern*, August 23, 1964; *International Affairs* (Moscow), No. 6, 1964, p. 17; *Zycie Warszawy*, September 5–6, 1964; *Neues Deutschland*, November 7, 1964.

9. Price, *op. cit.*, pp. 407, 412,

10. *Ibid.*, pp. 24–36.

11. *Ibid.*, p. 22.

12. See Joseph Barber, ed., *The Marshall Plan As American Policy, A Report on the Views of Community Leaders in Twenty-One Cities,* Council on Foreign Relations, New York City, 1948, pp. 19–20, 33 and 53, on American views regarding the desirability of making the Plan open to East Europe and the Soviet Union. For some of the underlying political thinking behind the Plan, see M. Beloff, *The United States and the Unity of Europe,* New York City, 1963, and particularly his account of the memorandum prepared within the Department of State in the early summer of 1947 by Charles Kindleberger, Harold B. van Cleveland, and Ben T. Moore (pp. 21–26), arguing the political case for the inclusion of East Europe and Germany in the Plan.

TABLE I: INTERNATIONAL TOURIST TRAVEL
Visitors by Country of Origin

West European Country	Population†	Travelers*	East European Country	Population†	Travelers*
Austria	7,128,000	2,004,485	Bulgaria	8,013,000	67,941
Belgium	9,222,000	2,315,907	Czechoslovakia	13,856,000	424,339
France	46,940,000	7,787,194	Germany, D.R. East Berlin	16,061,000† 1,064,000†	353,325
Germany, F.R.	54,766,000	11,257,704	Hungary	10,060,000	502,027
West Berlin	2,180,000				
Italy	50,003,000	1,331,556	Poland	30,324,000	248,509
Netherlands	11,797,000	3,036,061	Rumania	18,681,000	164,738
Spain	30,817,000	897,517	U.S.S.R.	221,465,000	198,611
Sweden	7,562,000	974,423	Yugoslavia	18,841,000	301,657

* Total of travelers from country of origin to all other countries listed on the table except travelers to Sweden and East Germany. The figures for travelers represent 1962 data with the exception of data on visitors *to* Czechoslovakia, Italy, and Poland which represent 1961 data, and Hungary for which complete data for 1963 have become available.
Source: UN Statistical Yearbook 1963, pp. 413–426, except for Hungary, based on *Statisztikai Havi Kozlemenyek,* June 1964.
† Population figures represent mid-1962 UN estimates with the exception of East Germany which is a mid-1961 estimate.
Source: UN Demographic Yearbook, 1962.
For German travelers to Poland (49,383) and Austria (3,725,339) no separate figures were given for East and West Germans. The figure for Poland has been added to the East German travelers and the figure for Austria to the West German travelers. Preliminary but incomplete data on East European travel for 1963 suggest a continuing growth in the number of East Europeans going abroad. The Hungarian figure for 1963 was not available on a country by country basis and hence in the totals the UN Statistical Yearbook 1963 was used.

TABLE II: FOREIGN TOURISTS (1962)
by Country Visited

Austria	5,679,575	Spain	7,332,780
Belgium	4,252,000	Bulgaria	324,041
France	5,975,000	Czechoslovakia	219,194
West Germany	5,322,670	Hungary	463,973
Greece	541,470	Poland*	375,450*
Ireland	2,104,200	Rumania	137,828
Italy	18,935,242	U.S.S.R.	909,604
Norway*	3,383,000*	Yugoslavia	1,241,875

* 1961 figures. Source: UN Statistical Yearbook 1963, pp. 413–426. Preliminary but incomplete data on East European travel for 1963 suggest continuing growth in the number of East Europeans going abroad.

Countries Trading	Total Trade 1958 Exports	Imports	1962 Exports	Imports	With the U. S. A. 1958 Exports	Imports	1962 Exports	Imports
U.S.S.R.	4298.5	4350.5	7033.7	6449.5	26.1	4.8	17.4	27.9
Albania	25.1	69.8	17.4	21.7	—	—	—	—
Bulgaria	374.9	366.6	608.0	653.8	—	—	1.0	—
Czechoslovakia	1513.4	1357.3	2914.0	3070.4	7.5	1.0	9.9	7.1
Germany, East	1890.2	1680.3	1815.4	1985.9	6.0	5.8	3.0	1.9
Hungary	679.8	629.4	835.2	857.5	2.1	1.7	1.6	.9
Poland	1060.4	1227.2	1646.9	1886.2	26.8	101.7	42.1	78.6
Rumania	469.0	482.4	685.3	780.2	.7	.7	.5	.5

Value of Trade in Million U.S. Dollars.
Source: Direction of Trade, Annual 1958-62, International Monetary Fund.

Countries Trading	Total Trade 1958 Exports	Imports	1962 Exports	Imports	With the U.S.S.R. 1958 Exports	Imports	1962 Exports	Imports
United States	17904.3	13410.2	21568.8	16477.6	3.4	17.5	19.7	15.9
United Kingdom	9392.1	10569.5	11059.2	12578.1	145.5	166.5	161.0	235.5
Germany, West*	8809.2	7413.2	13273.0	12391.6	72.2	92.0	206.8	215.0
France	5126.0	5612.7	7364.8	7521.3	75.9	94.9	138.1	110.7
Italy	2577.0	3215.6	4675.0	6085.2	31.1	40.4	102.3	166.3
Benelux	6263.2	6753.8	8908.7	9902.7	28.5	66.2	57.6	82.4

Value of Trade in Million U.S. Dollars.
Source: *Direction of Trade,* Annual 1958-1962. International Monetary Fund.

* The German figures for trade with East Europe include East Germany. (Source: *Aussenhandel Statistik des Deutschen Bundesamtes* (Wiesbaden), 1963. The percentage figures for 1963 are as follows: *U.S.*—Exp. .7, Imp. .5; *U.K.*—Exp. 3.5, Imp. 4.0; *W. Germany*—Exp. 4.5, Imp. 5.7; *France*—Exp. 3.6, Imp. 3.2; *Italy*—Exp. 5.8, Imp. 5.9; *Benelux*—Exp. 1.7, Imp. 2.4. (Source: *The Battle Act Report 1964,* pp. 65, 71.)

TRADE WITH THE WEST

| With the Common Market | | | | With the Rest of Europe | | | | Percentage of Total Trade with West | | | |
| 1958 | | 1962 | | 1958 | | 1962 | | 1958 | | 1962 | |
Exports	Imports	Exports	Imports	Exports	Imports	Exports	Imports	Exports	Imports	Exports	Imports
271.3	221.9	439.0	536.9	391.7	382.0	566.7	559.7	16.0	13.9	14.5	17.4
.5	1.9	1.5	5.6	.1	.2	.4	.1	2.4	3.0	10.9	26.2
22.6	25.1	57.1	54.2	9.2	9.0	30.0	27.8	8.5	9.3	14.5	12.5
109.8	122.2	151.5	157.1	91.9	108.4	104.7	129.1	13.8	17.1	12.1	14.1
251.8	250.0	48.5	41.3	100.0	122.7	114.1	124.3	19.0	22.5	9.1	8.4
74.5	72.4	91.1	119.6	65.1	67.4	83.6	80.6	20.8	22.5	21.1	23.5
120.1	138.1	171.1	134.4	188.2	208.7	271.1	262.2	31.6	36.5	29.4	25.2
55.8	51.3	128.6	149.2	29.0	25.8	58.6	78.9	18.2	16.1	27.4	28.0

TRADE WITH THE EAST

| With East Europe | | | | Percentage of Total | | | |
| 1958 | | 1962 | | 1958 | | 1962 | |
Exports	Imports	Exports	Imports	Exports	Imports	Exports	Imports
109.8	46.1	105.2	62.1	.6	.5	.5	.4
68.3	119.3	207.7	206.4	2.3	2.7	3.3	3.5
205.2	193.2	518.5	495.3	3.2	3.9	3.8	4.0
69.7	78.9	129.0	86.6	2.8	3.1	3.6	2.6
57.6	62.6	133.0	159.4	3.4	3.2	5.0	5.3
85.3	68.0	105.4	118.4	1.8	2.0	1.8	2.0

TABLE V: INTERCOMMUNIST TRADE (1962)

Countries	World Trade (Millions of U.S. $)		With the Soviet Union & Communist East Europe*		Percentage of Total	
	Total Exports	Total Imports	Exports	Imports	Exports	Imports
U.S.S.R.	7033.7	6449.5	3971.3	3587.6	56.4	55.6
Albania	17.4	21.7	15.0	12.7	86.2	58.5
Bulgaria	608.0	653.8	485.0	534.0	79.8	81.7
Czechoslovakia	2194.0	2070.4	1543.3	1429.4	70.3	69.0
East Germany	1815.4	1985.9	1536.3	1720.3	84.6	86.6
Hungary	835.2	857.5	596.5	599.7	71.4	69.9
Poland	1646.9	1886.2	958.9	1156.2	58.2	61.2
Rumania	685.3	780.2	448.6	498.0	65.5	63.8

* Excluding Yugoslavia.
Source: based on *Direction of Trade, Annual 1958–1962,* International Monetary Fund, Washington, D.C.
(Of the above, Rumania, Hungary, and Albania showed a decline in the level of inter-communist trade over the preceding year.)

TABLE VI: COCOM COUNTRIES TRADE WITH THE SOVIET UNION AND COMMUNIST EAST EUROPE
Industrial and Non-Industrial Items Compared—1962

(Figures in US $ pertain to *Imports* by COCOM countries from the Communist states and to *Imports* by the Soviet Union and the East European states from the COCOM countries.)

Items Traded	COCOM		Soviet Union	East Europe
	From the Soviet Union	From East Europe	From COCOM	From COCOM
Food, Beverages and Tobacco	108.2	388.3	40.5	164.1
Crude Materials	315.8	195.5	78.5	116.9
Mineral Fuels	220.2	222.8	.2	13.7
Fats and Oils	7.4	8.2	5.3	16.9
Chemicals	18.5	77.4	50.7	137.0
Manufactured Goods	166.2	255.0	276.1	415.5
Machinery	8.1	79.4	233.6	309.8
Transport Equipment	3.4	20.0	36.1	45.6

(COCOM Countries: USA, Canada, Japan, Benelux, Denmark, France, FRG, Greece, Italy, Norway, Portugal, Turkey and the UK. COCOM — The Coordinating Committee for strategic trade controls.)
Source: Adapted from pp. 122–25 of the *Joint Economic Committee* Report on Annual Economic Indicators for the USSR, Washington, 1964.

TABLE VII
SPAIN – YUGOSLAVIA – RUMANIA

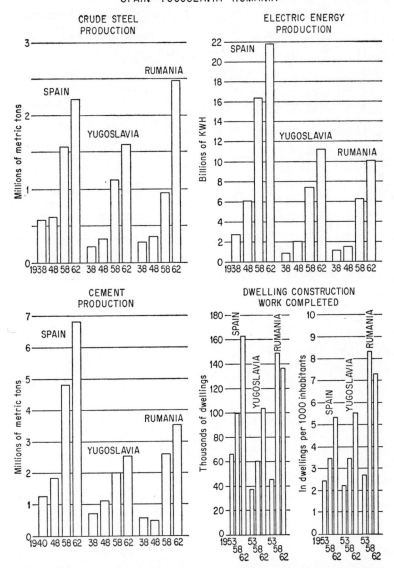

CRUDE STEEL PRODUCTION

ELECTRIC ENERGY PRODUCTION

CEMENT PRODUCTION

DWELLING CONSTRUCTION WORK COMPLETED

Note on Sources for Tables VII-XV. These tables were prepared by David L. Williams and were based on *Annual Bulletin of Housing and Building Statistics for Europe—1962* (U.N., Geneva, 1963); *United Nations Statistical Yearbook,* 1949–50, 1962; *United Nations Monthly Bulletin of Statistics,* March 1964, Vol. XVIII, No. 3.

TABLE VIII
SPAIN – YUGOSLAVIA – RUMANIA

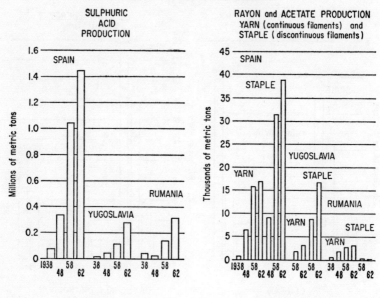

SULPHURIC
ACID
PRODUCTION

RAYON and ACETATE PRODUCTION
YARN (continuous filaments) and
STAPLE (discontinuous filaments)

TABLE IX
SPAIN – YUGOSLAVIA – RUMANIA

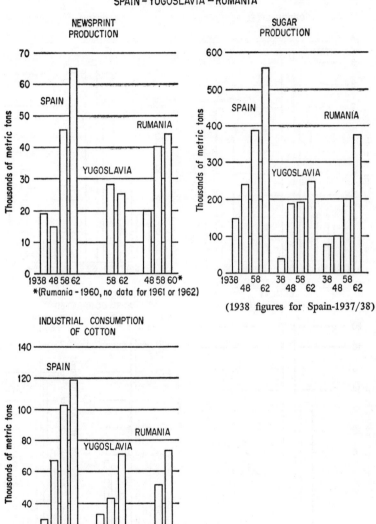

NEWSPRINT
PRODUCTION

*(Rumania - 1960, no data for 1961 or 1962)

SUGAR
PRODUCTION

(1938 figures for Spain-1937/38)

INDUSTRIAL CONSUMPTION
OF COTTON

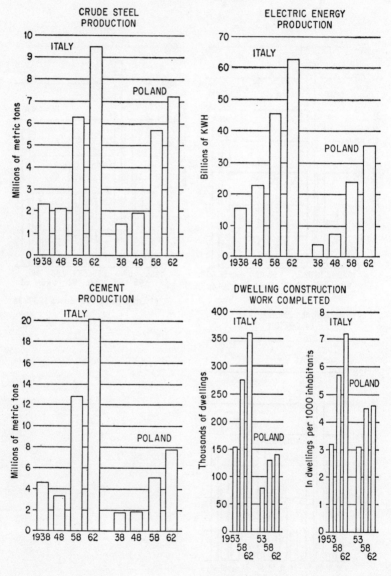

TABLE X
ITALY — POLAND

CRUDE STEEL
PRODUCTION

ITALY

POLAND

Millions of metric tons

1938 48 58 62   38 48 58 62

ELECTRIC ENERGY
PRODUCTION

ITALY

POLAND

Billions of KWH

1938 48 58 62   38 48 58 62

CEMENT
PRODUCTION

ITALY

POLAND

Millions of metric tons

1938 48 58 62   38 48 58 62

DWELLING CONSTRUCTION
WORK COMPLETED

ITALY

POLAND

Thousands of dwellings

1953 58 62   53 58 62

ITALY

POLAND

In dwellings per 1000 inhabitants

1953 58 62   53 58 62

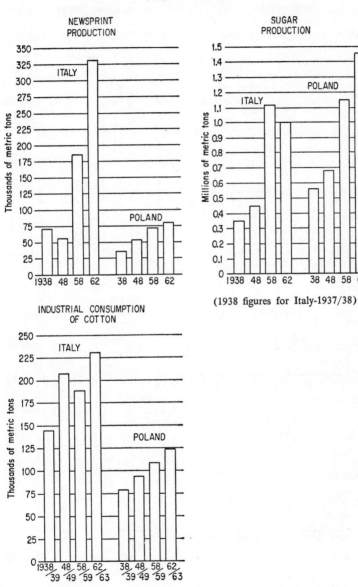

TABLE XI
ITALY — POLAND

NEWSPRINT
PRODUCTION

Thousands of metric tons

ITALY

POLAND

1938 48 58 62   38 48 58 62

SUGAR
PRODUCTION

Millions of metric tons

POLAND

ITALY

1938 48 58 62   38 48 58 62

(1938 figures for Italy-1937/38)

INDUSTRIAL CONSUMPTION
OF COTTON

Thousands of metric tons

ITALY

POLAND

1938 48 58 62   38 48 58 62
/39 /49 /59 /63   /39 /49 /59 /63

193

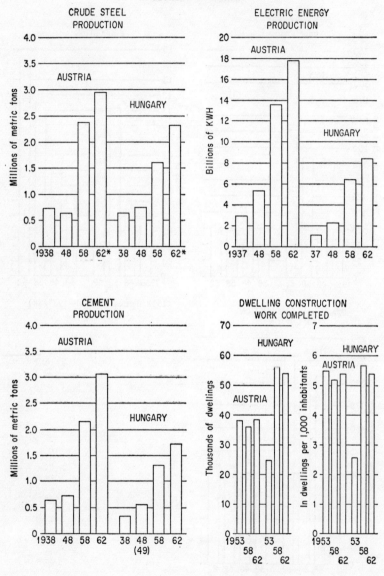

TABLE XII
AUSTRIA — HUNGARY

CRUDE STEEL
PRODUCTION

ELECTRIC ENERGY
PRODUCTION

CEMENT
PRODUCTION

DWELLING CONSTRUCTION
WORK COMPLETED

TABLE XIII
AUSTRIA – HUNGARY

SULPHURIC ACID PRODUCTION
(Production in terms of 100% H_2SO_4)

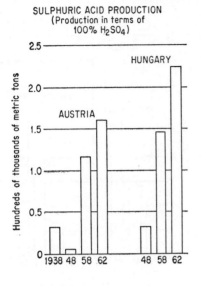

RAYON AND ACETATE PRODUCTION,
YARN (continuous filaments)
AND STAPLE (discontinuous filaments)

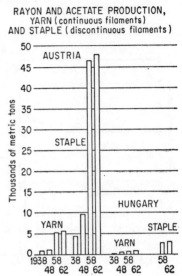

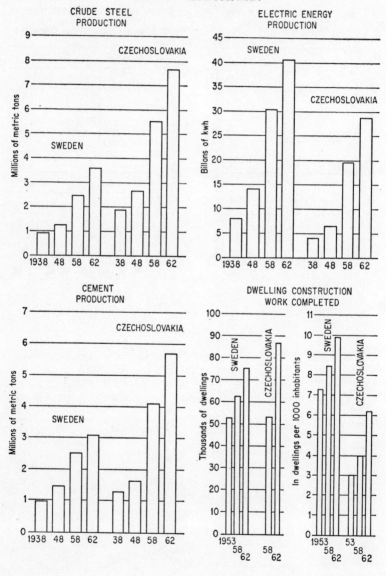

TABLE XIV

SWEDEN – CZECHOSLOVAKIA

CRUDE STEEL PRODUCTION

ELECTRIC ENERGY PRODUCTION

CEMENT PRODUCTION

DWELLING CONSTRUCTION WORK COMPLETED

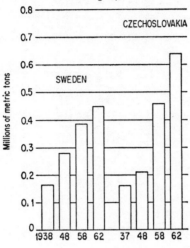

TABLE XV
SWEDEN - CZECHOSLOVAKIA

SULPHURIC ACID PRODUCTION
(Production in terms of
100 % $H_2 SO_4$)

TABLE XVI: THE ECONOMIC POTENTIAL OF FRANCE, THE UNITED KINGDOM, AND *UNITED GERMANY**

1962	France	United Kingdom	United Germany, of which:		
				West Germany	*East Germany*
Population**	46,998,000	53,441,000	74,049,000	56,947,000	17,102,000
Steel	17,200,000 tons	20,300,000 tons	36,222,000 tons	32,600,000 tons	3,622,000 tons
Pig Iron	14,200,000 tons	13,900,000 tons	26,275,000 tons	24,200,000 tons	2,075,200 tons
Coal	52,400,000 tons	200,600,000 tons	143,675,000 tons	141,100,000 tons	2,575,000 tons
Electric Energy	83 billion kwh	157 billion kwh	180 billion kwh	135 billion kwh	45 billion kwh
Petroleum	2,371,000 tons	113,000 tons	8,337,000 tons	6,776,000 tons	1,561,000 tons
Cement	16,700,000 tons	14,200,000 tons	34,032,000 tons	28,600,000 tons	5,432,000 tons
Sulphuric Acid	2,208,000 tons	2,772,000 tons	3,798,000 tons	3,096,000 tons	3,798,708 tons

* Source of figures for East Germany: *1963 Statistisches Jahrbuch der Deutschen Demokratischen Republik.* Source for all other figures: *Ekonomicheskoe Polozhenie Kapitalisticheskikh Stran* (supplement to "Mirovaia Ekonomika i Mezhdunarodnïe Otnosheniia" of August, 1964).

** 1962 estimates. Source: U.N. *Statistical Yearbook,* 1963.

Index

ABOUT THE AUTHOR

Zbigniew Brzezinski is Director of the Research Institute on Communist Affairs at Columbia University and is also a consultant to the Department of State. He is the author of several books, including *The Soviet Bloc—Unity and Conflict*, and most recently a co-author of *Political Power: USA/USSR*, published in 1964 by Viking. He is a recipient of the Junior Chamber of Commerce Award as one of the ten outstanding young men of 1963.

COUNCIL PUBLICATIONS

FOREIGN AFFAIRS (quarterly), edited by Hamilton Fish Armstrong.

THE UNITED STATES IN WORLD AFFAIRS (annual). Volumes for 1931, 1932 and 1933, by Walter Lippmann and William O. Scroggs; for 1934–1935, 1936, 1937, 1938, 1939, and 1940, by Whitney H. Shepardson and William O. Scroggs; for 1945–1947, 1947–1948 and 1948–1949, by John C. Campbell; for 1949, 1950, 1951, 1952, 1953 and 1954, by Richard P. Stebbins; for 1955, by Hollis W. Barber; for 1956, 1957, 1958, 1959, 1960, 1961, 1962 and 1963, by Richard P. Stebbins.

DOCUMENTS ON AMERICAN FOREIGN RELATIONS (annual). Volume for 1952 edited by Clarence W. Baier and Richard P. Stebbins; for 1953, and 1954, edited by Peter V. Curl; for 1955, 1956, 1957, 1958 and 1959, edited by Paul E. Zinner; for 1960, 1961, 1962 and 1963, edited by Richard P. Stebbins.

POLITICAL HANDBOOK AND ATLAS OF THE WORLD (annual), edited by Walter H. Mallory.

REMNANTS OF EMPIRE: The United Nations and the End of Colonialism, by David W. Wainhouse.

THE EUROPEAN COMMUNITY AND WORLD TRADE, by Randall Hinshaw

THE FOURTH DIMENSION OF FOREIGN POLICY: Educational and Cultural Affairs, by Philip Coombs.

JAPAN AND THE UNITED STATES IN WORLD TRADE, by Warren S. Hunsberger.

AMERICAN AGENCIES INTERESTED IN INTERNATIONAL AFFAIRS (Fifth Edition), compiled by Donald Wasson.

FOREIGN AFFAIRS BIBLIOGRAPHY 1952–1962, by Henry L. Roberts.

THE DOLLAR IN WORLD AFFAIRS, An Essay in International Financial Policy, by Henry G. Aubrey.

ON DEALING WITH THE COMMUNIST WORLD, by George F. Kennan.

FOREIGN AID AND FOREIGN POLICY, by Edward S. Mason

THE SCIENTIFIC REVOLUTION AND WORLD POLITICS, by Caryl P. Haskins.

AFRICA: A Foreign Affairs Reader, edited by Philip W. Quigg.

THE PHILIPPINES AND THE UNITED STATES: Problems of Partnership, by George E. Taylor.

SOUTHEAST ASIA IN UNITED STATES POLICY, by Russell H. Fifield.

UNESCO: ASSESSMENT AND PROMISE, by George N. Shuster.

THE PEACEFUL ATOM IN FOREIGN POLICY, by Arnold Kramish.

THE ARABS AND THE WORLD: Nasser's Arab Nationalist Policy, by Charles D. Cremeans.

TOWARD AN ATLANTIC COMMUNITY, by Christian A. Herter.

THE SOVIET UNION, 1922–1962: A Foreign Affairs Reader, edited by Philip E. Mosely.

THE POLITICS OF FOREIGN AID: American Experience in Southeast Asia, by John D. Montgomery.

SPEARHEADS OF DEMOCRACY: Labor in the Developing Countries, by George C. Lodge.

LATIN AMERICA: Diplomacy and Reality, by Adolf A. Berle.

THE ORGANIZATION OF AMERICAN STATES AND THE HEMISPHERE CRISIS, by John C. Dreier.

THE UNITED NATIONS: Structure for Peace, by Ernest A. Gross.

THE LONG POLAR WATCH: Canada and the Defense of North America, by Melvin Conant.

ARMS AND POLITICS IN LATIN AMERICA (Revised Edition), by Edwin Lieuwen.

THE FUTURE OF UNDERDEVELOPED COUNTRIES: Political Implications of Economic Development (Revised Edition), by Eugene Staley.

SPAIN AND DEFENSE OF THE WEST: Ally and Liability, by Arthur P. Whitaker.

SOCIAL CHANGE IN LATIN AMERICA TODAY: Its Implications for United States Policy, by Richard N. Adams, John P. Gillin, Allan R. Holmberg, Oscar Lewis, Richard W. Patch, and Charles W. Wagley.

FOREIGN POLICY: THE NEXT PHASE: The 1960s (Revised Edition), by Thomas K. Finletter.

DEFENSE OF THE MIDDLE EAST: Problems of American Policy (Revised Edition), by John C. Campbell.

COMMUNIST CHINA AND ASIA: Challenge to American Policy, by A. Doak Barnett.

FRANCE, TROUBLED ALLY: De Gaulle's Heritage and Prospects, by Edgar S. Furniss, Jr.

THE ATLANTIC POLICY STUDIES

In 1963, on the basis of a grant from the Ford Foundation, the Council on Foreign Relations undertook a program of twelve major studies of the future of the Atlantic Community, known as the Atlantic Policy Studies. Zbigniew K. Brzezinski's study of East-West relations in Europe and American policy, which appears in this volume, is the second of these studies to be published.

The Atlantic Policy Studies were undertaken out of a conviction that a searching examination of United States relations with, and policies toward, Western Europe is urgently needed. The studies are an attempt to come to grips with basic questions about the future of America's Atlantic relations.

The studies are policy-oriented, seeking not only to describe and forecast but also to prescribe. Each of the twelve studies is the responsibility of its author, but will consider its special problems in the light of the general aim of the program as a whole. The program is under the guidance of a Steering Committee, of which Charles M. Spofford is chairman.

The Atlantic Policy Studies are divided into four broad categories, dealing respectively with the external environment of the West; with problems of military strength and organization; with economic relations among the Atlantic countries and between them and less developed countries; and with Atlantic political relations.

Dr. Brzezinski's book is the first of two studies of the Atlantic world's external environment. A second, by Theodore Geiger of the National Planning Association, will examine the nature of the great transition now going on throughout Asia, Africa and Latin America, and its implications for the future of relations with the Western world.

Two studies of Atlantic military problems are included in the series. Henry A. Kissinger's *The Troubled Partnership: A Reappraisal of the Atlantic Alliance,* was published by McGraw-Hill in April, 1965. A book by Hedley Bull of London University will examine further the military-political problems of the alliance in the areas of nuclear weapons, arms control, and strategic doctrine.

Economic problems both within the Atlantic area and between the Atlantic nations and the rest of the world are examined in four separate studies. One, by John O. Coppock of Stanford University, will consider the principal problems of agricultural policy and trade within the Atlantic area. A second, by Richard N. Cooper of Yale University, will examine international financial arrangements and monetary institutions among the Atlantic nations, and prescribe policies for the future in this area. Trade arrangements and economic integration within the Atlantic Community are the subject of a third economic study, by Bela Balassa of Yale University, in collaboration with a group of economists from the United States, Europe, Canada and Japan. John Pincus of the RAND Corporation has undertaken a study of economic relations, trade and aid, between the industrial nations and the less developed countries.

Political relations among the Atlantic nations are the subject of four studies. Miriam Camps of Chatham House and the Council on Foreign Relations is preparing a volume on the future of European unity. Hans Speier of the RAND Corporation and the Council on Foreign Relations has undertaken a study of the implications of German foreign policy for the United States. Stanley Hoffmann of Harvard University will give a series of lectures at the Council in the spring of 1965, which will review the principal constraints, particularly the domestic constraints, on United States action in Atlantic affairs. His lectures will be published as a volume in the Atlantic Policy Series. A fourth political volume, by the Director of the Atlantic Policy Studies, will be addressed to the question of the future shape of political relations among the Atlantic countries.

Harold van B. Cleveland
Director, Atlantic Policy Studies
Council on Foreign Relations